Contents

Vichyssoise

This classic summer soup was created in the 1920s by Louis Diat, chef at the New York Ritz-Carlton.

ingredients

SERVES FOUR TO SIX

- 50g/2oz/¼ cup unsalted (sweet) butter
- 450g/1lb leeks, white parts only, thinly sliced
- 3 large shallots, sliced
- 250g/9oz floury potatoes (King Edward or Maris Piper), peeled and cut into chunks
- 1 litre/1¾ pints/4 cups light chicken stock or water
- 300ml/½ pint/1¼ cups double (heavy) cream
- iced water (optional)
- lemon or lime juice (optional)
- salt and ground black pepper
- chopped chives, to garnish

1 Melt the butter in a heavy pan and cook the leeks and shallots gently, covered, for 15–20 minutes, until soft.

2 Add the potato chunks and cook for a few minutes. Stir so they do not stick.

3 Stir in the stock or water and add salt and pepper to taste. Bring to the boil, then reduce the heat and partly cover the pan. Simmer for 15 minutes, or until the potatoes are soft.

4 Cool, then process the soup until smooth in a blender or food processor. Strain the soup into a bowl and stir in the cream. Taste and adjust the seasoning with salt and pepper and add a little iced water to thin down the soup if the consistency appears to be too thick.

5 Chill the soup for at least 4 hours or until very cold. Taste the chilled soup for seasoning and add a squeeze of lemon of lime juice, if required. Pour the soup into bowls and sprinkle with the chopped chives to garnish. Serve immediately.

cook's tip

Deep-fried shredded leek may be used to garnish the soup, as an alternative to the chopped chives.

NUTRITIONAL INFORMATION: Energy 547kcal/2260kJ; Protein 4.6g; Carbohydrate 17.7g, of which sugars 6.8g; Fat 51.4g, of which saturates 31.7g; Cholesterol 129mg Calcium 79mg; Fibre 3.6g; Sodium 103mg.

Yogurt Soup with Chilli Salsa

Charred salmon adds a smoky taste to complement the refreshing flavours in this soup.

ingredients

SERVES FOUR

- 3 medium cucumbers
- 300ml/½ pint/1½ cups Greek (US strained plain) yogurt
- 250ml/8fl oz/1 cup vegetable stock, chilled
- 120ml/4fl oz/½ cup crème fraîche
- 15ml/1 tbsp chopped fresh chervil
- 15ml/1 tbsp chopped fresh chives
- 15ml/1 tbsp chopped fresh flat leaf parsley
- 1 small red chilli, seeded and very finely chopped
- a little oil, for brushing
- 225g/8oz salmon fillet, skinned and cut into 8 thin slices
- salt and ground black pepper
- fresh chervil or chives, to garnish

1 Peel two of the cucumbers and halve them lengthways. Scoop out and discard the seeds and chop the flesh. Purée in a blender, then add the yogurt, stock, crème fraîche, chervil, chives and seasoning, and process until smooth. Chill.

2 Cut the remaining cucumber into small neat dice. Mix with the parsley and chilli to make the salsa. Chill.

3 Brush a griddle pan or a large, heavy frying pan with oil and heat until very hot.

4 Sear the salmon slices for 1–2 minutes on each side, until tender and charred.

5 Ladle the chilled soup into soup bowls. Top with two slices of the salmon, then pile a generous portion of salsa into the centre of each. Garnish with the chervil or chives and serve immediately.

variation

For a vegetarian alternative, replace the salmon with halved cherry tomatoes and diced halloumi cheese.

NUTRITIONAL INFORMATION: Energy 226kcal/942kJ; Protein 15.8g; Carbohydrate 9.1g, of which sugars 5.9g; Fat 14.4g, of which saturates 2.3g; Cholesterol 29mg; Calcium 177mg; Fibre 0.6g; Sodium 91mg.

Chilled Cucumber and Prawn Soup

This delicious and light chilled soup is the perfect way to celebrate an occasion in summer.

1 Melt the butter in a pan and cook the shallots and garlic over a low heat until soft but not coloured. Add the cucumber and cook until tender. Stir in the milk, bring to boiling point, then lower the heat and simmer for 5 minutes.

2 Pour the soup into a blender or food processor and purée until very smooth. Season with salt and ground white pepper to taste.

3 Pour the soup into a large bowl and leave to cool. When cool, stir in the prawns, chopped herbs and cream. Cover, transfer to the refrigerator and chill for at least 2 hours.

4 To serve, ladle the soup into four individual bowls. Top each portion with a dollop of crème fraîche, if using.

5 Arrange a prawn as a garnish over the edge of each dish. Scatter over a little extra chopped dill and tuck two or three chives under the prawns on the edge of the bowls to garnish. Serve at once.

cook's tip

Reheat gently for hot soup, but do not boil.

NUTRITIONAL INFORMATION: Energy 412kcal/1704kJ; Protein 14.2g; Carbohydrate 6g, of which sugars 6g; Fat 37g, of which saturates 23g; Cholesterol 206mg; Calcium 184mg; Fibre 0.2g; Sodium 197mg.

Chilled Almond Soup

This chilled Moorish soup is a perfect balance of almonds, garlic and vinegar, in a smooth purée.

ingredients

SERVES SIX

- 115g/4oz day-old white bread
- 115g/4oz/1 cup blanched almonds
- 2 garlic cloves, sliced
- 75ml/5 tbsp olive oil
- 25ml/1½ tbsp sherry vinegar
- salt and ground black pepper

For the garnish

- toasted flaked (sliced) almonds
- green and black grapes, halved and seeded
- chopped fresh chives

1 Break the bread into small pieces in a large glass bowl. Pour in 150ml/¼ pint/⅔ cup cold water, leave the bread to soak for about 5 minutes, then, using a fork, squeeze out the water until it is dry. Set aside until needed.

2 Put the blanched almonds and garlic in a food processor or blender and process until very finely ground. Add the soaked and dried white bread and process again until the mixture is thoroughly combined.

3 Continue to process the mixture, gradually adding the oil until the mixture forms a smooth thick paste. Add the sherry vinegar, followed by 600ml/1 pint/2½ cups cold water, and process until the mixture is smooth and free from any lumps.

4 Transfer the soup to a bowl. Season with plenty of salt and pepper, adding a little more water if the soup is very thick. Cover with clear film (plastic wrap) and chill for at least 2 hours.

5 Ladle the soup into bowls. Scatter the almonds, halved grapes and chopped chives over to garnish.

cook's tip

To accentuate the flavour of the almonds, dry roast them in a frying pan until they are lightly browned before grinding them.

NUTRITIONAL INFORMATION: Energy 245kcal/1017kJ; Protein 5.7g; Carbohydrate 10.8g, of which sugars 1.3g; Fat 20.2g, of which saturates 2.2g; Cholesterol 0mg; Calcium 67mg; Fibre 1.7g; Sodium 102mg.

Chilled Roasted Pepper Soup

To preserve the maximum flavour, serve this soup very cold, but not over-chilled.

ingredients

SERVES FOUR

- 1 onion, quartered
- 4 garlic cloves, unpeeled
- 2 red (bell) peppers, seeded and quartered
- 2 yellow (bell) peppers, seeded and quartered
- 30ml/2 tbsp olive oil
- grated rind and juice of 1 orange
- 200g/7oz can chopped tomatoes
- 600ml/1 pint/2½ cups cold water
- salt and ground black pepper
- 30ml/2 tbsp chopped fresh chives, to garnish (optional)

For the hot Parmesan toast

- 1 medium baguette
- 50g/2oz/¼ cup butter
- 175g/6oz Parmesan cheese

1 Preheat the oven to 200°C/400°F/Gas 6. Put the onion, garlic and peppers in a roasting pan. Drizzle the oil over the vegetables and mix well, then turn the pieces of pepper skin side up. Roast for 25–30 minutes, until slightly charred. Cool slightly.

2 Squeeze the garlic flesh into a food processor or blender. Add the roasted vegetables, orange rind and juice, tomatoes and water. Process until the mixture is smooth, then press through a sieve (strainer) into a bowl. Season the mixture well and chill for about 30 minutes.

3 Make the Parmesan toasts when you are ready to serve the soup. Preheat the grill (broiler) to high. Tear the baguette in half lengthways, then tear it across to give four large pieces. Spread with butter.

4 Pare most of the Parmesan into thin slices or shavings using a swivel-bladed vegetable knife or a small paring knife, then finely grate the remainder.

Arrange the sliced Parmesan on the toasts. Transfer to a large baking sheet or grill (broiling) pan and toast under the grill for a few minutes, until the topping is well browned.

5 Ladle the soup into bowls and sprinkle with chives, if using, and plenty of freshly ground black pepper. Serve with the Parmesan toast.

NUTRITIONAL INFORMATION: Energy 678kcal/2842kJ; Protein 28.7g; Carbohydrate 71.2g, of which sugars 17.1g; Fat 32.9g, of which saturates 16.8g; Cholesterol 70mg; Calcium 671mg; Fibre 5.9g; Sodium 1182mg.

Chilled Tomato and Pepper Soup

This recipe was inspired by the Spanish gazpacho but here the ingredients are cooked then chilled.

ingredients

SERVES FOUR

- 2 red (bell) peppers, halved
- 45ml/3 tbsp olive oil
- 1 onion, finely chopped
- 2 garlic cloves, crushed
- 675g/1½lb ripe tomatoes
- 150ml/¼ pint/⅔ cup red wine
- 600ml/1 pint/2½ cups vegetable stock
- salt and ground black pepper
- chopped fresh chives, to garnish

For the croûtons

- 2 slices day-old white bread, crusts removed
- 60ml/4 tbsp olive oil

1 Cut each pepper half into quarters and seed. Place skin side up on a grill (broiling) pan and cook until the skins have charred. Transfer to a bowl and cover with a plate.

2 Heat the oil in a large pan. Add the onion and garlic and cook until soft. Remove the skin from the peppers and chop them. Chop the tomatoes.

3 Add the peppers and tomatoes to the pan, then cover and cook gently for 10 minutes. Add the red wine and cook for a

further 5 minutes, then add the stock and simmer for 20 minutes.

4 To make the croûtons, cut the bread into cubes. Heat the oil in a small frying pan, add the bread and fry until golden.

Drain the croûtons well on kitchen paper, cool, then store in an airtight box.

5 Process the soup in a blender or food processor until the mixture is smooth. Pour into a clean glass or ceramic bowl and leave to cool thoroughly before chilling for at least 3 hours. When the soup is cold, season to taste with salt and pepper.

6 Serve the soup topped with the croûtons and garnished with the chopped fresh chives.

NUTRITIONAL INFORMATION: Energy 292kcal/1216kJ; Protein 3.4g; Carbohydrate 18.8g, of which sugars 11.8g; Fat 20.4g, of which saturates 3g; Cholesterol 0mg; Calcium 40mg; Fibre 3.5g; Sodium 92mg.

Chilled Tomato and Basil Soup

This fresh tomato soup is bursting with the delicious flavours of garlic and aromatic basil.

ingredients

SERVES FOUR

- 15ml/1 tbsp olive oil
- 1 onion, finely chopped
- 1 garlic clove, crushed
- 600ml/1 pint/2½ cups vegetable stock
- 900g/2lb tomatoes, roughly chopped
- 20 fresh basil leaves
- a few drops of balsamic vinegar
- juice of ½ lemon
- 150ml/¼ pint/⅔ cup natural (plain) yogurt
- sugar and salt, to taste

For the garnish

- 30ml/2 tbsp natural (plain) yogurt
- 8 small basil leaves
- 10ml/2 tsp basil flowers, all green parts removed

1 Heat the oil in a large, heavy pan and add the finely chopped onion and garlic. Fry over a medium heat in the oil for 2–3 minutes, until soft and transparent, but not browned, stirring occasionally.

2 Add 300ml/½ pint/1¼ cups of the vegetable stock and the roughly chopped tomatoes to the pan. Bring to the boil, then lower the heat and simmer the mixture for about 15 minutes. Stir it occasionally to prevent it from sticking to the base of the pan.

3 Allow the mixture to cool slightly, then transfer it to a food processor and process until smooth. Press through a sieve (strainer) placed over a bowl and discard the tomato skins and seeds remaining in the sieve.

4 Return the mixture to the food processor and add the remainder of the stock, half the basil leaves, the vinegar, lemon juice and yogurt. Season with sugar and salt to taste. Process the mixture until smooth. Pour the soup into a bowl and leave to chill.

5 Before serving, shred the remaining basil leaves and add them to the soup. Pour the soup into bowls. Garnish each bowl with yogurt, basil leaves and basil flowers.

cook's tip

If you can't find basil flowers, use chopped leaves instead.

NUTRITIONAL INFORMATION: Energy 117kcal/491kJ; Protein 4.4g; Carbohydrate 16.3g, of which sugars 14.8g; Fat 4.4g, of which saturates 0.9g; Cholesterol 1mg; Calcium 100mg; Fibre 2.3g; Sodium 55mg.

Tomato and Peach Jus with Prawns

The jus, which is the basis of this soup, is made from the juices extracted from tomatoes and peaches.

ingredients

SERVES SIX

- 1.2kg/2½lb large tomatoes
- 1.5kg/3¼lb ripe peaches
- 30ml/2 tbsp white wine vinegar
- 1 lemon grass stalk, crushed and chopped
- 2.5cm/1in piece fresh root ginger, grated
- 1 bay leaf
- 150ml/¼ pint/⅔ cup water
- 18 tiger prawns (jumbo shrimp), shelled with tails on
- olive oil, for brushing
- salt and ground black pepper
- fresh coriander (cilantro) and 2 tomatoes, peeled, seeded and diced, to garnish

1 Peel the tomatoes and peaches and cut into chunks. Put into a food processor and purée them. Stir in the vinegar and seasoning.

2 Line a large bowl with muslin (cheesecloth). Pour the purée into the bowl, gather up the ends of the muslin and tie tightly. Use the string to suspend the muslin bag over the bowl and leave at room temperature for 3 hours or until about 1.2 litres/2 pints/5 cups juice have drained through the cloth.

3 Meanwhile, put the lemon grass, ginger and bay leaf into a pan with the water, and simmer for 5–6 minutes. Set aside to cool.

4 When the mixture is cool, strain through a sieve into the tomato and peach juice and chill in the refrigerator for at least 4 hours.

5 Slit the prawns down their curved sides, cutting about three-quarters of the way through and keeping their tails intact. Open them out flat.

6 Heat a griddle or frying pan and brush with a little oil. Sear the prawns for 1–2 minutes on each side, until they are tender and slightly charred. Pat the prawns dry on kitchen paper to remove any remaining oil. Cool, but do not place in the refrigerator.

7 When ready to serve, ladle the soup into bowls and place three prawns in each portion.

8 Add some torn coriander leaves and diced tomato to each bowl, to garnish.

NUTRITIONAL INFORMATION: Energy 188kcal/797kJ; Protein 12.7g; Carbohydrate 25.2g, of which sugars 25.2g; Fat 4.8g, of which saturates 0.8g; Cholesterol 98mg; Calcium 71mg; Fibre 5.8g; Sodium 116mg.

Classic Gazpacho

This soup is a blend of tomatoes, peppers and garlic sharpened with sherry vinegar and olive oil.

ingredients

SERVES FOUR

- 1.3–1.6kg/3–3½lb ripe tomatoes
- 1 green (bell) pepper, seeded and roughly chopped
- 2 garlic cloves, finely chopped
- 2 slices day-old bread, crusts removed
- 60ml/4 tbsp extra virgin olive oil
- 60ml/4 tbsp sherry vinegar
- 150ml/¼ pint/⅔ cup tomato juice
- 300ml/½ pint/1¼ cups iced water
- salt and ground black pepper
- ice cubes, to serve (optional)

For the garnishes

- 30ml/2 tbsp olive oil
- 2–3 slices day-old bread, diced
- 1 small cucumber, peeled and finely diced
- 1 small onion, finely chopped
- 1 red (bell) and 1 green (bell) pepper, seeded and diced

1 Skin the tomatoes, then quarter them and remove the cores and seeds, saving the juices. Put the pepper in a food processor or blender and process for a few seconds. Add the tomatoes, reserved juices, garlic, bread, oil and vinegar and process. Add the tomato juice and blend to combine.

2 Season the soup to taste, then pour into a large bowl, cover with clear film (plastic wrap) and chill for at least 12 hours.

3 Prepare the garnishes. Heat the olive oil in a frying pan and fry the bread cubes for 4–5 minutes until golden brown and crisp. Drain well on kitchen paper, then arrange in a small dish. Place each of the remaining garnishes in separate small dishes.

4 Just before serving, dilute the soup with the ice-cold water. The consistency should be thick but not too stodgy. If you like, stir in a few ice cubes, then spoon into bowls and serve with the garnishes.

cook's tip

Make this soup for a light lunch or a simple supper.

NUTRITIONAL INFORMATION: Energy 356kcal/1494kJ; Protein 7.6g; Carbohydrate 41.9g, of which sugars 21.5g; Fat 18.8g, of which saturates 2.9g; Cholesterol 95mg; Calcium 90mg; Fibre 6.7g; Sodium 346mg.

Avocado Soup with Cumin

This soup, known as green gazpacho, was invented in Andalusia in southern Spain.

ingredients

SERVES FOUR

- 3 ripe avocados
- 1 bunch spring onions (scallions), white parts only, trimmed and roughly chopped
- 2 garlic cloves, chopped
- juice of 1 lemon
- 1.5ml/¼ tsp ground cumin
- 1.5ml/¼ tsp paprika
- 450ml/¾ pint/scant 2 cups fresh chicken stock, cooled, and all fat skimmed off
- 300ml/½ pint/1¼ cups iced water
- salt and ground black pepper
- roughly chopped fresh flat leaf parsley, to garnish

1 Starting half a day, or several hours, ahead to allow time for chilling, put the flesh of one avocado in a food processor or blender. Add the spring onions, garlic and lemon juice and purée until there is a smooth mixture.

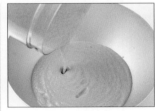

2 Add the second avocado and purée, then the third, with the spices and seasoning. Purée until smooth.

3 Gradually add the chicken stock. Pour the soup into a metal bowl and chill.

4 To serve the soup, stir in the iced water, then season to taste with plenty of salt and black pepper. Divide among four soup bowls. Garnish each bowl with some chopped parsley and serve immediately.

cook's tip

When avocados are plentiful, peel them, remove their stones (pits) and mash the flesh with lemon juice. Freeze in small containers. Thaw to make soups or dips.

NUTRITIONAL INFORMATION: Energy 148kcal/613kJ; Protein 1.9g; Carbohydrate 2.2g, of which sugars 1.1g; Fat 14.6g, of which saturates 3.1g; Cholesterol 0mg; Calcium 18mg; Fibre 2.9g; Sodium 6mg.

Avocado and Lime Soup

Inspired by guacamole, the popular avocado dip, this creamy soup relies on good-quality avocados.

SERVES FOUR

- 3 ripe avocados
- juice of 1½ limes
- 1 garlic clove, crushed
- handful of ice cubes, crushed
- 400ml/14f oz/1⅔ cups vegetable stock, chilled
- 400ml/14f oz/1⅔ cups milk, chilled
- 150ml/¼ pint/⅔ cup sour cream, chilled
- few drops of Tabasco
- salt and ground black pepper
- fresh coriander (cilantro), to garnish
- extra virgin olive oil, to serve

For the salsa

- 4 tomatoes, peeled, seeded and finely diced
- 2 spring onions (scallions), finely chopped
- 1 green chilli, seeded and finely chopped
- 15ml/1 tbsp chopped fresh coriander (cilantro)
- juice of ½ lime

1 Prepare the salsa first. Mix all the ingredients and season well. Chill until required.

2 Halve and stone (pit) the avocados. Scoop the flesh out of the avocado skins and place in a food processor or blender.

Add the lime juice, garlic, ice cubes and 150ml/¼ pint/⅔ cup of the chilled vegetable stock.

3 Process the soup until smooth. Pour into a bowl and stir in the remaining stock, milk, sour cream, Tabasco and seasoning. Cover and chill for no longer than 2 hours, or the avocado will discolour.

4 Serve the soup in four bowls or glasses and spoon a little salsa on top of each. If you like, serve small portions of the soup and take the bowl, the salsa and the olive oil to the table. Add a spoonful of the salsa and a splash of olive oil to each portion and garnish with a few coriander leaves.

NUTRITIONAL INFORMATION: Energy 335kcal/1390kJ; Protein 7.3g; Carbohydrate 12g, of which sugars 10.6g; Fat 28.9g, of which saturates 10g; Cholesterol 28mg; Calcium 176mg; Fibre 4.7g; Sodium 76mg.

Chilled Pea and Ham Soup

This simple soup is light and refreshing. Frozen petits pois produce a better flavour than canned.

ingredients

SERVES SIX

- 25g/1oz/2 tbsp butter
- 1 leek, sliced
- 1 garlic clove, crushed
- 450g/1lb/4 cups frozen petits pois (baby peas)
- 1.2 litres/2 pints/5 cups vegetable stock
- small bunch of chopped chives
- 300ml/½ pint/1¼ cups double (heavy) cream
- 90ml/6 tbsp Greek (US strained plain) yogurt
- 4 slices prosciutto, chopped
- salt and ground black pepper
- fresh chives, to garnish

1 Melt the butter in a pan. Add the leek and garlic, cover and cook gently for 4–5 minutes, until softened.

2 Stir in the petits pois, vegetable stock and chives. Bring slowly to the boil, then simmer for 5 minutes.

3 Cool the soup. Process the soup in a food processor or blender until smooth. Pour into a bowl, stir in the cream and season. Set aside to chill for at least 2 hours.

4 Ladle the soup into bowls and add a spoonful of Greek yogurt to each. Sprinkle the prosciutto over the top and garnish with chives.

cook's tip

- Use kitchen scissors to trim and cut the prosciutto straight into the soup, so that the pieces fall neatly.

- For a garnish, cut five lengths of chives, then use another chive to tie them together. Lay this on top of the soup.

cook's tip

Using frozen petits pois cuts out the work of shelling fresh peas. They taste better and are more tender, too.

NUTRITIONAL INFORMATION: Energy 386kcal/1610kJ; Protein 20.6g; Carbohydrate 32.8g, of which sugars 4.5g; Fat 20.1g, of which saturates 6.9g; Cholesterol 53mg; Calcium 47mg; Fibre 5.3g; Sodium 682mg.

Chilled Coconut Soup

This soup is cooling in hot weather. It is excellent to refresh the palate before the main course.

ingredients

SERVES SIX

- 1.2 litres/2 pints/5 cups milk
- 225g/8oz/2⅔ cups desiccated (dry unsweetened shredded) coconut
- 400ml/14fl oz/1⅔ cups coconut milk
- 400ml/14fl oz/1⅔ cups chicken stock
- 200ml/7fl oz/scant 1 cup double (heavy) cream
- 2.5ml/½ tsp salt
- 2.5ml/½ tsp ground white pepper
- 5ml/1 tsp caster (superfine) sugar
- fresh coriander (cilantro) leaves, to garnish

1 Pour the milk into a large pan. Bring it to the boil, stir in the coconut, lower the heat and allow to simmer for 30 minutes. Spoon the mixture into a food processor and process until smooth. This may take a while – up to 5 minutes – so pause frequently and take care to scrape down the sides of the bowl.

2 Rinse the pan to remove any coconut that remains, pour in the processed mixture and add the coconut milk. Stir in the chicken stock. (Home-made stock is best, if available, as it will give a far better flavour than a stock cube.)

3 Stir in the cream, salt, pepper and sugar. Bring to the boil, then lower the heat and cook for at least 10 minutes.

4 Reserve a few coriander leaves, then chop the rest finely and stir into the soup. Pour into a large bowl, cool, then cover and chill.

5 Before serving, check the seasoning and adjust if needed. Serve in chilled bowls, garnished with the coriander leaves.

cook's tip

If you want a lighter soup, omit the cream and use light coconut milk.

NUTRITIONAL INFORMATION: Energy 597kcal/2474kJ; Protein 10.8g; Carbohydrate 16.9g, of which sugars 16.9g; Fat 54.7g, of which saturates 40.8g; Cholesterol 69mg; Calcium 317mg; Fibre 6.7g; Sodium 188mg.

Iced Melon Soup

Use a variety of melons for this soup. Try a mix of Charentais and Ogen or cantaloupe and Galia.

ingredients

SERVES SIX TO EIGHT

- 2.25kg/5lb very ripe melon
- 45ml/3 tbsp orange juice
- 30ml/2 tbsp lemon juice
- fresh mint sprigs, to garnish

For the melon and mint sorbet

- 25g/1oz/2 tbsp sugar
- 120ml/4fl oz/½ cup water
- 2.25kg/5lb very ripe melon
- juice of 2 limes
- 30ml/2 tbsp chopped fresh mint

1 To make the melon and mint sorbet, put the sugar and water into a pan and heat gently until the sugar dissolves. Bring to the boil and simmer for 4–5 minutes, then remove from the heat and leave to cool.

2 Halve the melon. Scrape out the seeds, then cut it into large wedges and cut the flesh out of the skin. Weigh about 1.5kg/3–3½lb melon.

3 Purée the melon in a food processor with the cooled syrup and lime juice.

4 Stir in the mint and pour the melon mixture into an ice-cream maker. Churn, following the manufacturer's instructions, or until the sorbet is smooth and firm. Alternatively, pour the mixture into a freezer-proof container and freeze until ice crystals form around the edges of the container.

5 Transfer to a food processor or blender and process until smooth. Repeat the freezing and processing stage two or three times then freeze until the sorbet is firm.

6 To make the chilled melon soup, prepare the melon as in step 2 and purée it in a food processor or blender. Pour the purée into a bowl then add the orange and lemon juice. Mix together well. Place the soup in the refrigerator for 30–40 minutes, but do not chill it for too long, as this will dull its delicate flavour.

7 Ladle the soup into six or eight bowls and add a large scoop of the sorbet to each. Garnish with mint leaves and serve at once.

NUTRITIONAL INFORMATION: Energy 150kcal/636kJ; Protein 2.9g; Carbohydrate 35.3g, of which sugars 35.3g; Fat 0.6g, of which saturates 0g; Cholesterol 0mg; Calcium 75mg; Fibre 2.3g; Sodium 175mg.

Chilled Spicy Mango Soup

Mangoes may seem an unusual choice for a savoury soup, but this really is a delicious invention.

ingredients

SERVES FOUR

- 2 ripe mangoes
- 15ml/1 tbsp gram flour
- 120ml/4fl oz/½ cup natural (plain) yogurt
- 900ml/1½ pints/3¾ cups cold or chilled water
- 2.5ml/½ tsp grated fresh root ginger
- 2 fresh red chillies, seeded and finely chopped
- 30ml/2 tbsp olive oil
- 2.5ml/½ tsp mustard seeds
- 2.5ml/½ tsp cumin seeds
- 8 curry leaves
- salt and ground black pepper
- fresh mint leaves, shredded, and natural (plain) yogurt, to garnish

1 Peel the mangoes, remove the stones (pits) and cut the flesh into chunks. Purée in a food processor or blender until the mixture is smooth. Pour into a large, heavy pan and stir in the gram flour, yogurt, water, fresh root ginger and chillies. Bring the mixture slowly to the boil, stirring occasionally.

2 Simmer for 4–5 minutes until thickened slightly, then set aside off the heat.

3 Heat the oil in a frying pan over a medium to low heat. Add the mustard seeds and cook for a few seconds until they begin to pop, then add the cumin.

4 Add the curry leaves and cook for 5 minutes. Stir the spice mixture into the soup, return the pan to the heat and cook for a further 10 minutes.

5 Press through a sieve (strainer), if you like, then season to taste with salt and freshly ground black pepper. Leave the soup to cool, then chill for 1 hour.

6 Ladle the soup into bowls, and top each with yogurt. Garnish with shredded mint.

NUTRITIONAL INFORMATION: Energy 83kcal/354kJ; Protein 3g; Carbohydrate 14.4g, of which sugars 12.7g; Fat 2g, of which saturates 0.5g; Cholesterol 0mg; Calcium 72mg; Fibre 2g; Sodium 28mg.

Chilled Cherry Soup

Cherry soup is popular in Eastern Europe and is one of the glories of the Hungarian table.

ingredients

SERVES SIX

- 1kg/2¼lb fresh, frozen or canned sour cherries, such as Morello or Montmorency, pitted
- 175–250g/6–9oz/about 1 cup sugar, to taste
- 1–2 cinnamon sticks, each about 5cm/2in long
- 750ml/1¼ pints/3 cups dry red wine
- 5ml/1 tsp almond extract, or to taste
- 250ml/8fl oz/1 cup single (light) cream
- 250ml/8fl oz/1 cup sour cream or crème fraîche

1 Place the pitted cherries, 250ml/8fl oz/1 cup water, the sugar, cinnamon sticks and wine in a large, heavy pan. Bring to the boil then reduce the heat and simmer for about 20–30 minutes, until the cherries are just tender. Remove the pan from the heat and transfer the mixture to a large glass bowl.

2 Stir the desired quantity of almond extract into the soup and leave it to cool. Then cover the soup and chill it thoroughly.

3 In a bowl, stir a few tablespoons of single cream into the sour cream or crème fraîche to thin it, then stir in the rest until the mixture is smooth. Stir half the cream into the soup and chill. Chill the remaining cream.

4 To serve, ladle the soup into small bowls and swirl in the remaining cream.

variations

· When plums, greengages and damsons are in season, they can be used as good alternatives to the cherries.

· For a lower-fat alternative, use natural (plain) yogurt instead of cream and crème fraîche. Or replace with half-fat crème fraîche.

NUTRITIONAL INFORMATION: Energy 484kcal/2037kJ; Protein 3.7g; Carbohydrate 64.1g, of which sugars 64.1g; Fat 16.3g, of which saturates 10.3g; Cholesterol 48mg; Calcium 125mg; Fibre 1g; Sodium 53mg.

Carrot and Orange Soup

This traditional bright and summery soup is always popular for its wonderful creamy consistency.

ingredients

SERVES FOUR

- 50g/2oz/¼ cup butter
- 3 leeks, sliced
- 450g/1lb carrots, sliced
- 1.2 litres/2 pints/5 cups chicken or vegetable stock
- rind and juice of 2 oranges
- 2.5ml/½ tsp freshly grated nutmeg
- 150ml/¼ pint/⅔ cup Greek (US strained plain) yogurt
- salt and ground black pepper
- fresh sprigs of coriander (cilantro), to garnish

1 Melt the butter in a large pan. Add the leeks and carrots and stir well, coating the vegetables with the butter. Cover and cook gently for about 10 minutes, until the vegetables are beginning to soften but not to colour.

2 Pour in the stock and the orange rind and juice. Add the nutmeg and season to taste with salt and pepper. Bring to the boil, lower the heat, cover and simmer for about 40 minutes, or until the vegetables are tender.

3 Leave to cool slightly, then purée the soup in a food processor or blender until it is very smooth.

4 Return the soup to the pan and add 30ml/2 tbsp of the yogurt, then taste the

soup and check the seasoning, adding more salt and pepper if necessary. Reheat gently.

5 Ladle the soup into warm bowls and add a swirl of yogurt to each. Sprinkle the fresh sprigs of coriander over each bowl to garnish, and serve immediately.

cook's tip

Use a good, home-made chicken or vegetable stock for this recipe if you can, for the best results.

NUTRITIONAL INFORMATION: Energy 206kcal/856kJ; Protein 5g; Carbohydrate 15.8g, of which sugars 14.2g; Fat 14.4g, of which saturates 8.3g; Cholesterol 27mg; Calcium 111mg; Fibre 5.8g; Sodium 131mg.

Cream of Parsnip Soup

This delicious soup combines robustly flavoured parsnips with cumin and coriander.

ingredients

SERVES SIX

- 900g/2lb parsnips
- 50g/2oz/¼ cup butter
- 1 onion, chopped
- 2 garlic cloves, crushed
- 10ml/2 tsp ground cumin
- 5ml/1 tsp ground coriander
- about 1.2 litres/2 pints/5 cups hot chicken stock
- 150ml/¼ pint/⅔ cup single (light) cream
- salt and ground black pepper
- chopped fresh chives or parsley and/or croûtons, to garnish

1 Peel and thinly slice the parsnips. Heat the butter in a large, heavy pan and add the parsnips and onion with the crushed garlic. Cook gently for a few minutes until the vegetables are softened but not coloured, stirring them occasionally to prevent them sticking. Make sure that the garlic does not burn.

2 Add the cumin and coriander to the vegetable mixture and cook, stirring, for 1–2 minutes. Then gradually stir in the hot chicken stock and bring to the boil, stirring.

3 Cover the pan and simmer the soup for about 20 minutes, or until the parsnips are soft. Purée the soup; adjust the texture with extra stock or water if it seems too thick.

4 Add the cream and check the seasoning, then reheat the soup gently without boiling.

5 Serve immediately, sprinkled with chopped chives or parsley and/or croûtons, to garnish.

variations

A classic alternative is a mixture of parsnip and apple in equal proportions. Instead, you can also use a mixture of parsnips, carrots and swede (rutabaga).

NUTRITIONAL INFORMATION: Energy 325kcal/1355kJ; Protein 5.9g; Carbohydrate 32.1g, of which sugars 15.9g; Fat 20.1g, of which saturates 11.5g; Cholesterol 47mg; Calcium 138mg; Fibre 10.9g; Sodium 233mg.

Roasted Root Vegetable Soup

Roasting the vegetables gives this winter soup a wonderful depth of flavour.

ingredients

SERVES SIX

- 50ml/2fl oz/¼ cup olive oil
- 1 small butternut squash, peeled, seeded and cubed
- 2 carrots, cut into thick rounds
- 1 large parsnip, cubed
- 1 small swede (rutabaga), cubed
- 2 leeks, thickly sliced
- 1 onion, quartered
- 3 bay leaves
- 4 thyme sprigs, plus extra to garnish
- 3 rosemary sprigs
- 1.2 litres/2 pints/5 cups vegetable stock
- salt and freshly ground black pepper
- sour cream, to serve

1 Preheat the oven to 200°C/400°F/Gas 6. Pour the olive oil into a large bowl. Add the prepared squash, carrots, parsnip, swede, leeks and onion to the bowl and toss them thoroughly with a spoon until they are all evenly coated in the olive oil.

2 Spread out the vegetables in a single layer on one large or two small baking sheets. Tuck the bay leaves and the thyme and rosemary sprigs evenly among the vegetables.

3 Roast the vegetables for about 50 minutes until tender, turning them occasionally to make sure that they brown evenly. Remove from the oven, discard the herbs and transfer the vegetables to a large, heavy pan.

4 Pour the stock into the pan and bring to the boil. Season to taste and then simmer for 10 minutes. Transfer the soup to a food processor or blender (or use a hand blender) and process until smooth. Swirl in a spoonful of sour cream and serve.

cook's tip

Vary the vegetables used according to season.

NUTRITIONAL INFORMATION: Energy 65kcal/272kJ; Protein 2.5g; Carbohydrate 11.3g, of which sugars 8.8g; Fat 1.3g, of which saturates 0.3g; Cholesterol 0mg; Calcium 93mg; Fibre 4.4g; Sodium 13mg.

Leek and Potato Soup

Rocket adds its distinctive, peppery flavour to this version of a wonderfully satisfying soup.

ingredients

SERVES FOUR TO SIX

- 50g/2oz/4 tbsp butter
- 1 onion, chopped
- 3 leeks, chopped
- 2 floury potatoes, diced
- 900ml/1½ pints/3¾ cups light chicken stock or water
- 2 large handfuls rocket (arugula), roughly chopped
- 150ml/¼ pint/⅔ cup double (heavy) cream
- salt and ground black pepper
- garlic-flavoured ciabatta croûtons, to serve

1 Melt the butter in a large, heavy pan then add the onion, leeks and potatoes and stir well until the vegetables are coated in butter. Cook the ingredients over a high heat until they are sizzling and then reduce the heat to low.

2 Cover the pan and sweat the vegetables for 15 minutes. Pour in the stock or water and bring to the boil, then reduce the heat. Cover again and simmer for 20 minutes or until the vegetables are tender.

3 Press the soup through a sieve (strainer) or pass through a food mill and return to the rinsed-out pan. Add the chopped rocket to the pan and cook the soup gently, uncovered, for 5 minutes.

4 Stir in the cream, then season to taste and reheat gently. Ladle the soup into warmed soup bowls and serve with a generous scattering of garlic croûtons.

cook's tip

When puréeing the soup, a sieve (strainer) gives a good, smooth texture. A food processor or blender can make the soup glue-like.

variation

Try other peppery green leaves such as mizuna as alternatives to the rocket.

NUTRITIONAL INFORMATION: Energy 235kcal/972kJ; Protein 2.8g; Carbohydrate 9.4g, of which sugars 3.2g; Fat 20.9g, of which saturates 12.8g; Cholesterol 58mg; Calcium 75mg; Fibre 2.3g; Sodium 97mg.

Potato, Leek and Palm Soup

The distinctive flavour of palm hearts here is reminiscent of artichokes and asparagus.

ingredients

SERVES FOUR

- 25g/1oz/2 tbsp butter
- 10ml/2 tsp olive oil
- 1 onion, finely chopped
- 1 large leek, finely sliced
- 15ml/1 tbsp plain (all-purpose) flour
- 1 litre/1¾ pints/4 cups well-flavoured chicken stock
- 350g/12oz potatoes, peeled and cubed
- 2 x 400g/14oz cans hearts of palm, drained and sliced
- 250ml/8fl oz/1 cup double (heavy) cream
- salt and ground black pepper
- cayenne and chopped chives

1 Heat the butter and oil in a large pan over a low heat. Add the onion and leek and stir well until coated. Cover and cook for 5 minutes until softened and translucent.

2 Sprinkle the plain flour into the pan over the vegetables. Stir in and cook, still stirring constantly, for 1 minute.

3 Pour in the chicken stock and add the potatoes. Bring to the boil, stirring, then lower the heat and simmer for 10 minutes. Stir in the hearts of palm and the cream, and simmer gently for a further 10 minutes.

4 Process the soup in a food processor or blender until smooth. Pour it back into the rinsed-out pan and heat gently, adding a little water if necessary. The consistency should be thick but not too heavy. Do not allow to boil. Season with salt and ground black pepper.

5 Ladle the soup into warm bowls and garnish each with a pinch of cayenne and chopped chives. Serve immediately.

cook's tip

Serve with fresh bread for a really satisfying lunch.

NUTRITIONAL INFORMATION: Energy 486kcal/2013kJ; Protein 5.2g; Carbohydrate 25.1g, of which sugars 7.9g; Fat 41.2g, of which saturates 24.5g; Cholesterol 99mg; Calcium 147mg; Fibre 4.9g; Sodium 184mg.

Peanut and Potato Soup

In this Latin-American soup, peanuts are used as a thickening agent, with delicious results.

ingredients

SERVES SIX

- 60ml/4 tbsp groundnut (peanut) oil
- 1 onion, finely chopped
- 2 garlic cloves, crushed
- 1 red (bell) pepper, seeded and chopped
- 250g/9oz potatoes, peeled and diced
- 2 fresh red chillies, seeded and chopped
- 200g/7oz canned chopped tomatoes
- 150g/5oz/1¼ cups unsalted peanuts
- 1.5 litres/2½ pints/6¼ cups vegetable stock
- salt and ground black pepper
- 30ml/2 tbsp chopped fresh coriander (cilantro), to garnish

1 Heat the oil in a large heavy pan. Add the onion and cook for 5 minutes. Add the garlic, pepper, potatoes, chillies and tomatoes and cook for 5 minutes.

2 Meanwhile, toast the peanuts by gently cooking them in a large dry frying pan. Turn and stir the peanuts until they are evenly golden. Take care not to burn them.

3 Set 30ml/2 tbsp of the peanuts aside for garnish. Grind the remaining nuts in a food processor or blender. Add the vegetables and process until they are smooth. Return the mixture to the pan and stir in the stock. Bring to the boil, lower the heat and simmer for 10 minutes.

4 Pour the soup into six heated bowls. Garnish with a generous scattering of chopped coriander. Chop the reserved 30ml/2 tbsp peanuts and divide among the bowls.

variation

Replace the peanuts with crunchy and smooth peanut butter for the ideal texture.

NUTRITIONAL INFORMATION: Energy 260kcal/1079kJ; Protein 8g; Carbohydrate 14.7g, of which sugars 6.2g; Fat 19.2g, of which saturates 3.6g; Cholesterol 0mg; Calcium 30mg; Fibre 3g; Sodium 20mg.

Artichoke and Fennel Soup

Jerusalem artichokes are nutty and delicious in soup and bruschetta is an ideal accompaniment.

ingredients

SERVES SIX

- squeeze of lemon juice
- 450g/1lb Jerusalem artichokes, peeled and diced
- 65g/2½oz/5 tbsp butter
- 175g/6oz potatoes, diced
- 1 small onion, chopped
- 1 garlic clove, chopped
- 1 celery stick, chopped
- 1 small fennel bulb, chopped
- 1.2 litres/2 pints/5 cups vegetable stock
- 300ml/½ pint/1¼ cups double (heavy) cream
- pinch of grated nutmeg
- salt and ground black pepper
- basil leaves, to garnish

For the bruschetta

- 6 thick slices French bread
- 1 garlic clove
- 50g/2oz/¼ cup unsalted (sweet) butter
- 400g/14oz can artichoke hearts, drained and halved
- 45ml/3 tbsp tapenade
- 9 salted anchovy fillets, halved lengthways

1 Prepare a bowl of water with lemon juice. Add the Jerusalem artichokes to the water to prevent discoloration.

2 Melt the butter in a large pan. Drain the artichokes and add to the pan with the potatoes, onion, garlic, celery and fennel. Cook for 10 minutes, stirring occasionally, until softened but not coloured.

3 Add the stock, bring to the boil, and simmer for 10–15 minutes, until all the vegetables are soft.

4 Cool slightly, then purée until smooth. Add the cream and nutmeg and season well.

5 For the bruschetta, lightly toast the French bread on both sides. Rub generously with the garlic. Melt the butter in a small pan. Add the artichoke hearts and cook for 3–4 minutes, turning once.

6 Spread the tapenade on the toast and arrange the artichoke hearts on top. Top with the halved anchovy fillets and garnish with basil.

7 Reheat the soup without boiling, then ladle it into shallow bowls. Serve the bruschetta with the soup.

NUTRITIONAL INFORMATION: Energy 533kcal/2212kJ; Protein 7.2g; Carbohydrate 25.9g, of which sugars 4.3g; Fat 45.3g, of which saturates 27.1g; Cholesterol 114mg; Calcium 167mg; Fibre 3.4g; Sodium 787mg.

Curried Cauliflower Soup

This spicy, creamy soup is perfect on a winter's day served with bread and garnished with coriander.

ingredients

SERVES FOUR

- 750ml/1¼ pints/3 cups milk
- 1 large cauliflower
- 15ml/1 tbsp garam masala
- salt and ground black pepper
- coriander (cilantro) leaves, to garnish

cook's tip

There is no need to discard all the outer leaves from a cauliflower when making soup. Trim off any wilted or badly damaged green parts and stalks, and any very tough stalk. Then cut off the florets and dice the larger parts of the stalk. Thinly slice the leafy parts from around the sides. Add all these to the pan and they will add excellent flavour to the soup.

1 Pour the milk into a large, heavy pan and place over a medium heat. Using your hands or a knife, break the cauliflower into florets and add to the milk with the garam masala and season well with salt and pepper.

2 Bring the milk to the boil, then reduce the heat, partially cover the pan and simmer for about 20 minutes.

3 Let the mixture cool for a few minutes, then transfer to a food processor or blender and process until it is smooth (you may have to do this in two batches).

4 Return the cauliflower purée to the rinsed-out pan and heat gently, adjusting the seasoning. Ladle into four warm bowls and garnish with a few leaves of coriander and sprinkle with ground black pepper. Serve the soup immediately.

NUTRITIONAL INFORMATION: Energy 136kcal/575kJ; Protein 11.5g; Carbohydrate 13.3g, of which sugars 12g; Fat 4.6g, of which saturates 2.2g; Cholesterol 11mg; Calcium 259mg; Fibre 3.1g; Sodium 100mg.

Pumpkin and Coconut Soup

This winter soup is rich with coconut, which is balanced by an intriguing hint of sugar and spice.

4 Reheat the soup and taste it for seasoning, then ladle into bowls. Spoon a little rice on each portion and dust with ground cinnamon. Serve immediately, offering more rice at the table.

1 Using a small sharp knife, scrape away any seeds or strands of fibre from the pumpkin, cut off the peel and chop the flesh. Put the prepared pumpkin in a pan and add the stock, coconut milk, sugar and seasoning.

2 Bring to the boil, reduce the heat and cover. Simmer for about 20 minutes, until the pumpkin is tender. Purée the soup in a food processor or blender. Return it to the rinsed-out pan.

3 Place the rice in a pan and rinse it in several changes of cold water. Then drain in a sieve (strainer) and return it to the pan. Add plenty of fresh cold water to cover and bring to the boil. Stir, reduce the heat and simmer for 15 minutes, until the grains are tender. Drain.

variations

• *This soup would work equally well using butternut squash or any type of squash that is in season in place of the pumpkin, and brown rice in place of the white rice.*

• *Following the amount given here, you should have just enough of the white rice left over to serve as an accompaniment on the side, if you wish.*

NUTRITIONAL INFORMATION: Energy 148kcal/627kJ; Protein 8.8g; Carbohydrate 20.7g, of which sugars 13.5g; Fat 4g, of which saturates 2.3g; Cholesterol 11mg; Calcium 308mg; Fibre 2.8g; Sodium 81mg.

Aubergine and Mozzarella Soup

Gremolata, a classic Italian garnish combining garlic, lemon and parsley, enhances this creamy soup.

ingredients

SERVES SIX

- 30ml/2 tbsp olive oil
- 2 shallots, chopped
- 2 garlic cloves, chopped
- 1kg/2¼lb aubergines (eggplants) trimmed and roughly chopped
- 1 litre/1¾ pints/4 cups chicken stock
- 150ml/¼ pint/⅔ cup double (heavy) cream
- 30ml/2 tbsp chopped fresh parsley
- 175g/6oz mozzarella cheese, thinly sliced
- salt and ground black pepper

For the gremolata

- 2 garlic cloves, finely chopped
- grated rind of 2 lemons
- 60ml/4 tbsp chopped fresh parsley

1 Heat the oil in a large pan and add the shallots and garlic. Cook for 4–5 minutes, until softened. Add the aubergines and cook for about 25 minutes, stirring occasionally, until they are soft and browned.

2 Pour in the stock and bring to the boil. Reduce the heat, cover and simmer for about 5 minutes, until the aubergines are very soft. Leave the soup to cool slightly before processing.

3 Purée the soup in a food processor or blender until

smooth. Pour it back into the rinsed-out pan. Add the cream and seasoning to taste. Stir in the parsley and heat through.

4 Mix the garlic, grated lemon rind and parsley for the gremolata. Ladle the soup into

bowls and lay the mozzarella on top. Scatter with the gremolata and serve.

cook's tip

Buffalo mozzarella is the creamiest type. The large blocks of cheaper Danish mozzarella tend to be dense and rubbery and let down this delicious soup.

NUTRITIONAL INFORMATION: Energy 261kcal/1079kJ; Protein 7.5g; Carbohydrate 4.9g, of which sugars 4.3g; Fat 23.7g, of which saturates 13.1g; Cholesterol 5 mg; Calcium 137mg; Fibre 3.5g; Sodium 124mg.

Onion Soup with Chives

This wonderful soup has a deep, buttery flavour that is complemented by croûtons and chives.

ingredients

SERVES FOUR

- 115g/4oz/½ cup unsalted (sweet) butter
- 1kg/2¼lb onions, sliced
- 1 fresh bay leaf
- 105ml/7 tbsp dry white vermouth
- 1 litre/1¾ pints/4 cups good chicken or vegetable stock
- 150ml/¼ pint/⅔ cup double (heavy) cream
- a little lemon juice (optional)
- salt and ground black pepper
- chopped fresh chives, to garnish
- croûtons, to serve

1 Melt 75g/3oz/6 tbsp of the butter in a heavy pan. Set about 200g/7oz of the onions aside and add the rest to the pan with the bay leaf. Stir to coat in the butter, then cover and cook very gently for about 30 minutes. The onions should be very soft and tender, but they should not be browned.

cook's tip

This soup can be vegetarian or not, depending on the stock you decide to use.

2 Add the vermouth, increase the heat and boil rapidly until all the liquid has evaporated. Add the stock, about 5ml/1 tsp salt and pepper to taste. Bring to the boil, lower the heat and simmer for 5 minutes, then remove from the heat.

3 Let the soup cool, discard the bay leaf and process in a food processor or blender. Return the soup to the pan.

4 Meanwhile, melt the remaining butter in another pan and cook the remaining onions slowly, covered, until soft but not browned. Uncover and continue to cook gently until the onions are a golden yellow colour.

5 Add the cream to the soup and reheat it gently until hot, but do not allow it to boil. Taste and adjust the seasoning, adding a little lemon juice if liked. Add the buttery onions and stir for 1–2 minutes, then ladle the soup into four bowls. Sprinkle each bowl of soup with chopped chives and serve with croûtons.

NUTRITIONAL INFORMATION: Energy 233kcal/965kJ; Protein 7.2g; Carbohydrate 16.2g, of which sugars 12.3g; Fat 16g, of which saturates 5.2g; Cholesterol 27mg; Calcium 51mg; Fibre 3.3g; Sodium 398mg.

Sherried Onion Soup

The classic Spanish combination of onions, sherry and saffron is delicious in this golden soup.

ingredients

SERVES FOUR

- 40g/1½oz/3 tbsp butter
- 2 large onions, thinly sliced
- 1 small garlic clove, finely chopped
- pinch of saffron threads
- 50g/2oz blanched almonds, toasted and finely ground
- 750ml/1¼ pints/3 cups vegetable stock
- 45ml/3 tbsp fino sherry
- 2.5ml/½ tsp paprika
- salt and ground black pepper

For the garnish

- 30ml/2 tbsp flaked (sliced) almonds, toasted
- chopped fresh parsley

1 Melt the butter in a large, heavy pan over a low heat. Add the onions and chopped garlic and stir for about a minute to ensure that they are thoroughly coated in the melted butter.

2 Cover the pan and cook the onions very gently, stirring frequently, for about 20 minutes, until they are golden, but not browned.

3 Add the saffron threads to the pan and cook, uncovered, for 3–4 minutes. Add the

ground almonds and cook, stirring constantly, for a further 2–3 minutes.

4 Pour in the stock and sherry with 5ml/1 tsp salt and the paprika. Season with plenty of black pepper. Bring to the boil,

stirring, then lower the heat, cover the pan and simmer gently for about 10 minutes.

5 Pour the soup into a food processor or blender and process until smooth, then return it to the rinsed-out pan. Reheat gently, without allowing the soup to boil, stirring occasionally. Check the seasoning and adjust to taste.

6 Ladle the soup into bowls. Garnish with the almonds and parsley, then serve immediately.

NUTRITIONAL INFORMATION: Energy 255kcal/1054kJ; Protein 5.8g; Carbohydrate 11.5g, of which sugars 8.1g; Fat 19.6g, of which saturates 6.1g; Cholesterol 21mg; Calcium 82mg; Fibre 3.2g; Sodium 68mg.

Garlic Soup with Egg

Spanish soup and Italian polenta marry wonderfully well in this simple but tasty recipe.

ingredients

SERVES FOUR

- 15ml/1 tbsp olive oil
- 1 garlic bulb, unpeeled and broken into cloves
- 4 slices day-old ciabatta bread, broken into pieces
- 1.2 litres/2 pints/5 cups chicken stock
- pinch of saffron
- 4 poached eggs
- salt and ground black pepper
- chopped fresh parsley, to garnish

For the polenta

- 750ml/1¼ pints/3 cups milk
- 175g/6oz/1 cup quick-cook polenta
- 50g/2oz/¼ cup butter

1 Preheat the oven to 200°C/400°F/Gas 6. Brush the oil over a roasting pan, then add the garlic and bread and roast for about 20 minutes. Leave until cool enough to handle.

2 Meanwhile, make the polenta. Bring the milk to the boil in a large, heavy pan and gradually stir in the polenta. Cook, stirring constantly, for about 5 minutes, or according to the packet instructions, until the polenta begins to come away from the side of the pan.

3 Spoon the polenta on to a chopping board and spread out to about 1cm/½in thick. Allow to cool and set, then cut into 1cm/½in dice.

4 Squeeze the garlic cloves from their skins into a food processor. Add the dried bread and 300ml/½ pint/1¼ cups of the stock, then process until smooth. Pour into a pan. Pound the saffron in a mortar and stir in a little of the remaining stock, then add to the soup with enough of the remaining stock to thin the soup.

5 Melt the butter in a frying pan and cook the diced polenta over a high heat for 1–2 minutes, tossing all the time, until it begins to brown. Drain on kitchen paper.

6 Season the soup and reheat gently. Place a poached egg in the bottom of each of four bowls. Ladle the soup over the eggs, generously scatter polenta croûtons and parsley on top and serve.

NUTRITIONAL INFORMATION: Energy 415kcal/1731kJ; Protein 13.4g; Carbohydrate 43.9g, of which sugars 0.9g; Fat 20.8g, of which saturates 8.6g; Cholesterol 217mg; Calcium 57mg; Fibre 1.9g; Sodium 247mg.

Mushroom Soup with Croûtes

This classic soup is still a favourite, especially when it is served with crisp and garlicky croûtes.

ingredients

SERVES SIX

- 1 onion, chopped
- 1 garlic clove, chopped
- 25g/1oz/2 tbsp butter
- 450g/1lb/6 cups chestnut or brown cap (cremini) mushrooms, roughly chopped
- 15ml/1 tbsp plain (all-purpose) flour
- 45ml/3 tbsp dry sherry
- 900ml/1½ pints/3¾ cups vegetable stock
- 150ml/¼ pint/⅔ cup double (heavy) cream
- salt and ground black pepper
- sprigs of fresh chervil, to garnish

For the croûtes

- 15ml/1 tbsp olive oil, plus extra for brushing
- 1 shallot, chopped
- 115g/4oz/1½ cups button (white) mushrooms, chopped
- 15ml/1 tbsp chopped fresh parsley
- 6 brown cap (cremini) mushrooms
- 6 slices baguette
- 1 small garlic clove
- 115g/4oz/1 cup soft goat's cheese

1 Cook the onion and garlic in the butter for 5 minutes. Add the mushrooms, cover and cook for 10 minutes, stirring often. Stir in the flour and cook for 1 minute. Stir in the sherry and stock and bring to the boil, then simmer for 15 minutes. Cool slightly, then purée in a food processor or blender.

2 For the croûtes, heat the oil in a small pan. Add the shallot and button mushrooms and cook for 8–10 minutes. Drain and discard the liquid then transfer the mixture to a blender or food processor with the chopped fresh parsley. Process until finely chopped.

3 Brush the mushrooms with oil and grill (broil) under a hot grill (broiler) for 5–6 minutes. Toast the baguette, rub with the garlic and top with goat's cheese. Add the grilled mushrooms and fill these with the mushroom mixture.

4 Return the soup to the pan, stir in the cream and reheat gently. Float a croûte in each bowl and garnish with chervil.

NUTRITIONAL INFORMATION: Energy 368kcal/1533kJ; Protein 10.3g; Carbohydrate 25.1g, of which sugars 3.1g; Fat 25g, of which saturates 14.5g; Cholesterol 61mg; Calcium 99mg; Fibre 2.4g; Sodium 399mg.

30

Asparagus and Pea Soup

This bright and tasty summery soup is good to make when there is a glut of asparagus.

ingredients

SERVES SIX

- 350g/12oz asparagus
- 2 leeks
- 1 bay leaf
- 1 carrot, roughly chopped
- 1 celery stick, chopped
- few stalks of fresh parsley
- 1.75 litres/3 pints/7½ cups cold water
- 25g/1oz/2 tbsp butter
- 150g/5oz fresh garden peas
- 15ml/1 tbsp chopped fresh parsley
- 120ml/4 fl oz/½ cup double (heavy) cream
- grated rind of ½ lemon
- salt and ground black pepper
- shavings of Parmesan cheese, to serve

1 Cut the woody ends from the asparagus, then set the spears aside. Roughly chop the woody ends and place them in a large pan. Cut off and chop the green parts of the leeks and add to the asparagus stalks with the bay leaf, carrot, celery, parsley stalks and the cold water. Bring to the boil and simmer for about 30 minutes. Strain the stock and discard the cooked vegetables.

2 Cut the tips off the asparagus and set aside, then cut the stems into short pieces.

Finely chop the remainder of the leeks (the white parts).

3 Melt the butter in a large pan and add the leeks. Cook for 3–4 minutes until softened. Add the asparagus stems, peas and parsley. Pour in 1.2 litres/2 pints/5 cups of the asparagus stock. Boil, reduce the heat and cook for 6–8 minutes. Season.

4 Purée in a food processor or blender. Press through a fine sieve (strainer) into the pan. Add the cream and lemon rind.

5 Bring a small pan of water to the boil and cook the asparagus tips for 2–3 minutes or until they are tender. Drain and refresh them under cold water. Reheat the soup, but do not allow it to boil.

6 Ladle the soup into six warmed bowls and garnish with asparagus tips. Serve at once, with shavings of Parmesan cheese and plenty of ground black pepper.

NUTRITIONAL INFORMATION: Energy 184kcal/759kJ; Protein 4.9g; Carbohydrate 7.2g, of which sugars 4.4g; Fat 15.3g, of which saturates 9.1g; Cholesterol 36mg; Calcium 56mg; Fibre 3.9g; Sodium 39mg.

Courgette Soup with Cheese

This soup has a delicate colour, a rich and creamy texture and a subtle flavour.

ingredients

SERVES FOUR TO SIX

- 30ml/2 tbsp olive oil
- 5g/½oz/1 tbsp butter
- onion, roughly chopped
- 900g/2lb courgettes (zucchini), trimmed and sliced
- 5ml/1 tsp dried oregano
- about 600ml/1 pint/2½ cups vegetable or chicken stock
- 150g/4oz Dolcelatte cheese, rind removed, diced
- 300ml/½ pint/1¼ cups single (light) cream
- salt and ground black pepper
- fresh oregano and extra Dolcelatte, to garnish

1 Heat the oil and butter in a large pan until foaming. Add the onion and cook gently for about 5 minutes, stirring frequently, until softened but not brown.

2 Add the courgettes and oregano to the pan, with salt and pepper to taste. Cook over medium heat for 10 minutes, stirring frequently.

3 Pour in the stock and bring to the boil, stirring. Lower the heat, half cover the pan and simmer gently, stirring occasionally, for about 30 minutes. Stir in the diced Dolcelatte and heat gently, still stirring, until it has melted.

4 Process the soup in a food processor or blender until smooth, then press through a sieve (strainer) back into the rinsed-out pan.

5 Add two-thirds of the cream and stir over a low heat until hot, but be careful not to boil the soup. Check the consistency and add more stock if the soup seems too thick. Taste and adjust the seasoning.

6 Pour the soup into heated bowls. Swirl in the remaining cream and sprinkle with a little extra cheese. Garnish each portion with a few sprigs of oregano and serve.

variations

- If you prefer a more pronounced cheese flavour, use Gorgonzola instead of Dolcelatte.

- Try other cheeses to create subtly different flavours.

NUTRITIONAL INFORMATION: Energy 248kcal/1024kJ; Protein 8.5g; Carbohydrate 5.4g, of which sugars 4.8g; Fat 21.5g, of which saturates 11.7g; Cholesterol 7mg; Calcium 181mg; Fibre 1.6g; Sodium 266mg.

Celery Soup with Stilton

Stilton – known as the "king of English cheeses" – and celery are traditional partners.

ingredients

SERVES SIX

- 40g/1½oz/3 tbsp butter
- 1 large onion, finely chopped
- 1 potato, cut into small cubes
- 1 head of celery, thinly sliced
- 900ml/1½ pints/3¾ cups vegetable or chicken stock
- 100g/3¾oz Stilton cheese, crumbled
- 150ml/¼ pint/⅔ cup single (light) cream
- salt and ground black pepper

1 Melt the butter in a large pan and add the onion. Cook over a medium heat for 5 minutes, stirring occasionally, until soft but not browned.

2 Stir in the potato and celery and cook for a further 5 minutes until the vegetables soften and begin to brown.

3 Add the stock, bring to the boil, then cover the pan and simmer gently for about 30 minutes, until all the vegetables are very soft.

4 In a food processor or blender, purée about three-quarters of the soup until smooth, then return it to the pan with the rest of the soup. For a smoother soup, process a larger batch.

5 Bring the soup just to the boil, stirring all the time to prevent sticking, and season to taste with salt and ground black pepper.

6 Remove the pan from the heat and stir in the cheese, reserving a little for the garnish.

7 Stir in three-quarters of the cream, reserving just a little for garnish if you like, and reheat the soup gently, if necessary, without boiling.

8 Serve the soup topped with the reserved crumbled cheese and drizzled with the remaining single cream.

cook's tip

It is worth looking out for good quality Stilton that really shows off the rich, creamy texture and tang of the famous blue-veined cheese.

NUTRITIONAL INFORMATION: Energy 199kcal/826kJ; Protein 5.9g; Carbohydrate 7.5g, of which sugars 2.4g; Fat 16.2g, of which saturates 10.4g; Cholesterol 44mg; Calcium 117mg; Fibre 1.4g; Sodium 233mg.

Classic Tomato Soup

This creamy soup owes its excellent flavour to a mixture of fresh and canned tomatoes.

ingredients

SERVES FOUR TO SIX

- 25g/1oz/2 tbsp butter
- 1 onion, finely chopped
- 1 small carrot, finely chopped
- 1 celery stick, finely chopped
- 1 garlic clove, crushed
- 450g/1 lb ripe tomatoes, roughly chopped
- 400g/14oz can chopped tomatoes
- 30ml/2 tbsp tomato purée (paste)
- 30ml/2 tbsp sugar
- 600ml/1 pint/2½ cups chicken or vegetable stock
- 1 tbsp chopped fresh thyme or oregano leaves
- 600ml/1 pint/2½ cups milk
- salt and ground black pepper

1 Melt the butter in a large, heavy pan. Add the onion, carrot, celery and garlic. Cook over a medium heat for about 5 minutes, stirring occasionally, until soft and just beginning to turn brown.

2 Add the tomatoes, tomato purée, sugar, chicken or vegetable stock and herbs, retaining some to garnish.

3 Bring to the boil, then cover and simmer gently for about 20 minutes until all the vegetables are very soft.

4 In a food processor or blender, purée the mixture until smooth, then press it through a sieve (strainer) to remove the skins and seeds.

5 Return the sieved soup to the rinsed-out pan and stir in the milk. Reheat gently, but do not boil.

6 Stir the soup and season to taste with salt and ground black pepper. To serve, ladle the hot soup into four to six bowls and garnish each bowl with the remaining herbs.

cook's tips

· In summer it is practicable to use all fresh tomatoes, but do make sure they are really ripe and full of flavour.

· Tomatoes do ripen quickly but to help the process along, put one ripe tomato in a bowl with unripe tomatoes.

NUTRITIONAL INFORMATION: Energy 107kcal/447kJ; Protein 2.3g; Carbohydrate 11.4g, of which sugars 10.9g; Fat 6.1g, of which saturates 3.5g; Cholesterol 13mg; Calcium 50mg; Fibre 3.9g; Sodium 71mg.

Corn and Potato Chowder

This creamy, yet chunky, soup is filled with the sweet taste of corn and punchy Cheddar cheese.

ingredients

SERVES FOUR

- 1 onion, chopped
- 1 garlic clove, crushed
- 1 large potato, chopped
- 2 celery sticks, sliced
- 1 small green (bell) pepper, seeded, halved and sliced
- 30ml/2 tbsp sunflower oil
- 25g/1oz/2 tbsp butter
- 600ml/1 pint/2½ cups vegetable stock or water
- 300ml/½ pint/1¼ cups milk
- 200g/7oz can flageolet or cannellini beans
- 300g/11oz can corn
- good pinch of dried sage or a few small fresh sage leaves
- salt and ground black pepper
- Cheddar or Monterey Jack cheese, grated, to garnish

1 Put the onion, garlic, potato, celery and green pepper into a pan with the oil and butter.

2 Heat until sizzling, then reduce the heat to low. Cover and cook for 10 minutes, stirring now and then.

3 Pour in the vegetable stock or water, increase the heat and bring to the boil. Reduce the heat, cover again and simmer gently for about 15 minutes or until the vegetables are just tender but not so soft that they break up.

4 Add the milk, beans and corn, including the liquor from the cans. Stir in the sage and seasoning.

5 Heat until the mixture is simmering, then cook gently, uncovered, for about 5 minutes. Check the seasoning before ladling the chowder into four bowls, and adjust if necessary. Sprinkle each with some of the cheese and serve immediately.

NUTRITIONAL INFORMATION: Energy 320kcal/1347kJ; Protein 9.4g; Carbohydrate 43.2g, of which sugars 15.7g; Fat 13.5g, of which saturates 5g; Cholesterol 18mg; Calcium 119mg; Fibre 5g; Sodium 500mg.

Leek and Cheese Soup

This substantial Irish soup can be a good way to use up cheese left over from the cheeseboard.

ingredients

SERVES SIX

- 3 large leeks
- 50g/2oz/¼ cup butter
- 30ml/2 tbsp oil
- 115g/4oz farmhouse cheese, such as Cashel Blue
- 15g/½oz/2 tbsp plain (all-purpose) flour
- 15ml/1 tbsp wholegrain mustard, or to taste
- 1.5 litres/2½ pints/6¼ cups vegetable stock
- ground black pepper

For the garnish
- 50g/2oz cheese, grated
- chopped chives or chopped spring onion (scallion) greens

1 Slice the leeks thinly. Heat the butter and oil together in a large, heavy pan and add the leeks. Cover and cook gently over a low heat for 10–15 minutes, until the leeks are just softened and tender but not turning brown.

2 Grate the cheese coarsely and add it to the pan, stirring over a low heat, until it is melted. Add the flour and cook for 2 minutes, stirring constantly with a wooden spoon, then add ground black pepper and wholegrain mustard to taste.

3 Gradually add the stock, stirring constantly, and bring the soup to the boil.

4 Reduce the heat, cover and simmer gently for about 15 minutes. Check the seasoning.

5 Divide the soup among six bowls and serve garnished with the extra grated cheese and chives or spring onion greens. Offer plenty of fresh bread with the soup.

variation

Any melting cheese can be used in this recipe. To retain the Irish flavour, try Cooleeney, a soft white cheese from County Tipperary, or St Killian or Mileens, from West Cork.

NUTRITIONAL INFORMATION: Energy 187kcal/773kJ; Protein 5.6g; Carbohydrate 4.3g, of which sugars 1.9g; Fat 16.6g, of which saturates 8.6g; Cholesterol 32mg; Calcium 118mg; Fibre 1.8g; Sodium 407mg.

36

Garlic and Coriander Soup

A simple soup of Portuguese origin, this should be made with only the best ingredients.

ingredients

SERVES SIX

- 25g/1oz fresh coriander (cilantro), leaves and stalks chopped separately
- 1.5 litres/2½ pints/6¼ cups vegetable stock or water
- 5–6 plump garlic cloves, peeled
- 5ml/1 tsp vinegar
- 6 eggs
- 275g/10oz day-old bread, most of the crust removed, torn into bitesize pieces
- 90ml/6 tbsp extra virgin olive oil, plus extra to serve
- salt and ground black pepper

1 Place the coriander stalks in a pan. Add the stock or water and bring to the boil. Lower the heat, cover and simmer for 10 minutes. Process the soup in a food processor or blender and then press it through a sieve (strainer) back into the rinsed-out pan.

2 Crush the garlic with 5ml/1 tsp salt using a mortar and pestle or in a small bowl. Stir in 120ml/4fl oz/½ cup of the hot soup and then pour the mixture back in the pan to reheat gently.

3 Meanwhile, poach the eggs. Heat a large frying pan of water, adding the vinegar, until boiling. Crack an egg into a cup or saucer. Reduce the heat so that the water simmers, swirl the water and drop the egg into the middle of the swirl. Poach for 3–4 minutes, until just set.

4 Add the remaining eggs in the same way as Step 3 (cook them in two batches if the pan is too small to hold all six at once). Use a draining spoon to remove the eggs from the pan and when they are free of water

transfer them to a warmed plate. Trim off any untidy bits of egg white with kitchen scissors.

5 Bring the soup back to the boil and add seasoning. Stir in the chopped coriander leaves and remove from the heat.

6 Place the bread in six soup plates or bowls and drizzle the oil over it. Ladle in the soup and stir. Add a poached egg to each portion and serve immediately, offering olive oil at the table so that it can be drizzled over the soup to taste.

NUTRITIONAL INFORMATION: Energy 290kcal/1212kJ; Protein 10.9g; Carbohydrate 24.1g, of which sugars 1.4g; Fat 17.5g, of which saturates 3.1g; Cholesterol 190mg; Calcium 89mg; Fibre 1.2g; Sodium 310mg.

Roast Vegetable Medley

Winter meets summer in this soup of chunky roasted roots, served with hot, flavoured bread.

ingredients

SERVES FOUR

- 4 parsnips, quartered lengthways
- 2 red onions, cut into thin wedges
- 4 carrots, thickly sliced
- 2 leeks, thickly sliced
- 1 small swede (rutabaga), cut into chunks
- 4 potatoes, cut into chunks
- 60ml/4 tbsp olive oil
- few sprigs of fresh thyme
- 1 garlic bulb, broken into cloves, unpeeled
- 1 litre/1¾ pints/4 cups vegetable stock
- salt and ground black pepper
- fresh thyme sprigs, to garnish

For the sun-dried tomato bread

- 1 ciabatta loaf
- 75g/3oz/6 tbsp butter, softened
- 1 garlic clove, crushed
- 4 sun-dried tomatoes, finely chopped
- 30ml/2 tbsp chopped fresh parsley

1 Preheat the oven to 200°C/400°F/Gas 6. Cut the thick ends of the parsnip quarters into four, then place them in a large roasting pan. Add the onion wedges, carrot and leek slices, swede and potato chunks, and spread them all out in an even layer.

2 Drizzle the olive oil over the vegetables. Add the thyme and unpeeled garlic cloves. Toss well to coat and roast for 45 minutes, until all the vegetables are tender and slightly charred.

3 To make the sun-dried tomato bread, slice the loaf, without cutting right through. Mix the butter, garlic, sun-dried tomatoes and parsley. Spread the butter between the slices. Wrap in foil. Bake for 15 minutes, opening the foil for the last 4–5 minutes.

4 Discard the thyme from the vegetables. Squeeze the garlic from its skins over the vegetables and purée half the mixture with the stock. Pour into a pan. Add the remaining vegetables. Bring to the boil.

5 Ladle the soup into bowls and garnish with fresh thyme sprigs. Serve the hot bread with the soup.

NUTRITIONAL INFORMATION: Energy 511kcal/2146kJ; Protein 13.9g; Carbohydrate 72.6g, of which sugars 18.9g; Fat 20.4g, of which saturates 10.6g; Cholesterol 40mg; Calcium 218mg; Fibre 12.1g; Sodium 521mg.

Squash and Blue Cheese Soup

This soup is, in fact, a very liquid risotto and makes a very smart first course for a dinner party.

ingredients

SERVES FOUR

- 25g/1oz/2 tbsp butter
- 30ml/2 tbsp olive oil
- 2 onions, finely chopped
- ½ celery stick, finely sliced
- 1 small butternut squash, peeled, seeded and diced
- 15ml/1 tbsp chopped fresh sage
- 300g/11oz/1½ cups risotto or arborio rice
- 1.2 litres/2 pints/5 cups hot chicken stock
- 30ml/2 tbsp double (heavy) cream
- 30ml/2 tbsp olive oil
- 4 large fresh sage leaves
- salt and ground black pepper
- 115g/4oz blue cheese, finely diced

1 Place the butter and oil in a large, heavy pan and heat gently. Add the onions and celery and cook for 4–5 minutes over a low heat. Stir in the butternut squash and cook for a further 3–4 minutes, then add the chopped sage.

2 Add the rice and cook for 1–2 minutes, stirring, until the grains are slightly translucent. Add the chicken stock a ladleful at a time.

3 Cook until each ladleful of stock has been absorbed before adding another. Continue adding the stock in this way until you have a very wet rice mixture. Season then stir in the double cream.

4 Meanwhile, heat the oil in a frying pan and fry the sage leaves for a few seconds until crisp. Drain. Stir the blue cheese into the risotto soup and ladle it into bowls. Garnish with fried sage leaves.

variation

Experiment with different kinds of squash and with different blue cheeses to create adaptations of this soup according to season and what is available.

NUTRITIONAL INFORMATION: Energy 505kcal/2100kJ; Protein 9.2g; Carbohycrate 63.7g, of which sugars 5.7g; Fat 23g, of which saturates 8.3g; Cholesterol 26mg; Calcium 110mg; Fibre 2.7g; Sodium 91mg.

Sweet-and-Sour Borscht

This version of the classic Eastern European soup includes plenty of cabbage, tomato and potatoes.

ingredients

SERVES SIX

- 1 onion, chopped
- 1 carrot, chopped
- 4–6 raw or plain cooked beetroot (beets), 3–4 diced and 1–2 coarsely grated
- 400g/14oz can tomatoes
- 4–6 new potatoes, cut into bitesize pieces
- 1 small white cabbage, thinly sliced
- 1 litre/1¾ pints/4 cups vegetable stock
- 45ml/3 tbsp sugar
- 30–45ml/2–3 tbsp white wine vinegar or cider vinegar
- 45ml/3 tbsp chopped fresh dill, plus extra to garnish
- salt and ground black pepper
- sour cream, to garnish
- buttered rye bread, to serve

1 Put the onion, carrot, diced beetroot, tomatoes, potatoes and cabbage in a pan. Add the stock and bring to the boil. Reduce the heat and cover.

2 Simmer the soup for about 30 minutes, or until the potatoes are tender.

3 Add the grated beetroot, sugar and vinegar to the soup and continue to cook for 10 minutes.

variation

To make meat borscht, place 1kg/2¼ lb chopped beef in a pan. Add water to cover with 1 beef stock (bouillon) cube. Bring to the boil, reduce the heat and simmer until tender. Skim off fat, add vegetables and proceed as above.

4 Taste for a good sweet–sour balance and add more sugar and/or vinegar if necessary. Season to taste.

5 To serve, stir in the chopped dill and ladle the soup into six bowls. Garnish each portion with a generous spoonful of sour cream and with some more dill. Serve with plenty of buttered rye bread.

NUTRITIONAL INFORMATION: Energy 46kcal/196kJ; Protein 1.6g; Carbohydrate 9.8g, of which sugars 6.4g; Fat 0.4g, of which saturates 0.1g; Cholesterol 0mg; Calcium 22mg; Fibre 1.9g; Sodium 29mg.

Grandfather's Soup

This traditional Eastern European soup derives its name from the fact that it is easily digested!

1 In a large, heavy pan, cook the onion gently in the butter for 10 minutes, until golden.

2 Add the diced potatoes and cook for 2–3 minutes, then pour in the stock. Add the bay leaf, salt and pepper. Bring to the boil, then reduce the heat, cover and simmer for about 10 minutes.

3 For the noodles, sift the flour and salt into a bowl and rub in the butter. Add the parsley and egg and mix to a soft dough.

4 Drop half-teaspoonfuls of the dough into the simmering soup. Cover and simmer gently for a further 10 minutes. Ladle among four warmed soup bowls, sprinkle each bowl with the parsley, and serve with chunks of bread.

cook's tip

To get the correct texture for this soup, old, floury potatoes work best.

NUTRITIONAL INFORMATION: Energy 239kcal/1001kJ; Protein 5.5g; Carbohydrate 33.3g, of which sugars 5g; Fat 10.2g, of which saturates 5.7g; Cholesterol 69mg; Calcium 96mg; Fibre 2.3g; Sodium 157mg.

Spinach and Root Soup

This is a typical Russian soup, traditionally prepared when the first vegetables of the season appear.

ingredients

SERVES FOUR TO SIX

- 1 small turnip, cut into chunks
- 2 carrots, sliced or diced
- 1 small parsnip, cut into large dice
- 1 potato, peeled and diced
- 1 onion, chopped or cut into chunks
- 1 garlic clove, finely chopped
- ¼ celeriac bulb, diced
- 1 litre/1¾ pints/4 cups vegetable or chicken stock
- 200g/7oz spinach, washed and roughly chopped
- 1 small bunch fresh dill, chopped
- salt and ground black pepper

For the garnish

- 2–3 hard-boiled eggs, halved
- 1 lemon, cut into slices
- 250ml/8fl oz/1 cup sour cream
- 30ml/2 tbsp chopped fresh parsley and dill

1 Put the turnip, carrots, parsnip, potato, onion, garlic, celeriac and stock into a large, heavy pan. Bring the vegetables to the boil, then simmer for 25–30 minutes, or until the vegetables are very tender but not mushy.

2 Add the spinach to the pan and cook for 5 minutes, or until the spinach is tender but still green and leafy. Season.

3 Stir the dill into the soup, then ladle into four to six bowls and serve garnished with the egg halves, sliced lemon, sour cream and a sprinkling of parsley and dill.

cook's tip

Use a really good-quality stock for flavour.

NUTRITIONAL INFORMATION: Energy 229kcal/952kJ; Protein 7.8g; Carbohydrate 14.3g, of which sugars 9.2g; Fat 16.2g, of which saturates 8.7g; Cholesterol 133mg Calcium 197mg; Fibre 4.1g; Sodium 148mg.

Green Bean and Almond Soup

This tasty soup uses a mixture of fresh green vegetables with nuts in a delicious combination.

ingredients

SERVES EIGHT

- 225g/8oz green beans
- 1 garlic clove, roughly chopped
- 2 macadamia nuts or 4 almonds, finely chopped
- 1cm/½in cube shrimp paste
- 10–15ml/2–3 tsp coriander seeds, dry fried
- 15ml/1 tbsp sunflower oil
- 1 onion, finely sliced
- 400ml/14fl oz can reduced-fat coconut milk
- 2 bay leaves
- 8 thin lemon wedges
- 30ml/2 tbsp lemon juice
- 225g/8oz/4 cups beansprouts

1 Cut the beans into small pieces. Bring 1.2 litres/2 pints/5 cups water to the boil with a little salt. Add the beans and cook for 3–4 minutes. Drain, reserving the cooking water. Set the water and beans aside.

2 Finely grind the chopped garlic, the macadamia nuts or almonds, the shrimp paste and the coriander seeds to a paste using a mortar and pestle or in a food processor.

3 Heat the oil in a pan and fry the onion until browned. Remove with a slotted spoon. Add the nut paste to the pan and fry it for 2 minutes without allowing it to brown.

4 Add the reserved vegetable water and stir well. Add the coconut milk, bring to the boil and add the bay leaves. Reduce the heat and simmer, uncovered, for 15–20 minutes.

5 Just before serving, reserve a few green beans and some fried onion for garnish. Stir the rest into the soup and heat through without boiling.

6 Add the lemon wedges, lemon juice and seasoning to the soup and stir. Garnish each bowl with the reserved green beans, onion and beansprouts.

cook's tip
Lemon wedges can be served on the side if preferred.

variation
Any seasonal vegetables can be substituted for the beans.

NUTRITIONAL INFORMATION: Energy 51kcal/212kJ; Protein 2.2g; Carbohydrate 5.2g, of which sugars 4.2g; Fat 2.5g, of which saturates 0.4g; Cholesterol 3mg; Calcium 43mg; Fibre 1.2g; Sodium 84mg.

Potato Soup with Samosas

Soup and samosas are ideal partners. Here, bought samosas are given a clever flavour lift.

ingredients

SERVES FOUR

- 60ml/4 tbsp sunflower oil
- 10ml/2 tsp black mustard seeds
- 1 large onion, chopped
- 1 fresh red chilli, seeded and chopped
- 2.5ml/½ tsp ground turmeric
- 1.5ml/¼ tsp cayenne pepper
- 900g/2lb potatoes, cut into cubes
- 4 fresh curry leaves
- 750ml/1¼ pint/3 cups vegetable stock
- 225g/8oz spinach leaves, torn if large
- 400ml/14fl oz/1⅔ cups coconut milk
- handful of fresh coriander (cilantro) leaves
- salt and ground black pepper

For the garlic samosas

- 1 large garlic clove, crushed
- 25g/1oz/2 tbsp butter
- 4 vegetable samosas

1 Heat the oil in a large pan. Add the mustard seeds, cover and cook until they begin to pop. Add the onion and chilli and cook for 5–6 minutes.

2 Stir in the turmeric, cayenne, potatoes, curry leaves and stock. Bring to the boil, reduce the heat and cover the pan. Simmer for 15 minutes, stirring occasionally, until the potatoes are tender.

3 Meanwhile, prepare the samosas. Preheat the oven to 180°C/350°F/Gas 4.

4 Melt the butter with the garlic in a small pan, stirring and crushing the garlic into the butter to release the flavour.

5 Place the samosas on a baking tray or in an ovenproof dish. Brush them lightly with the butter on each side. Heat through in the oven for about 5 minutes, until they are piping hot.

6 Add the spinach to the soup and cook for 5 minutes. Stir in the coconut milk and cook for a further 5 minutes.

7 Season to taste with salt and pepper and add the coriander leaves before ladling the soup into four bowls. Serve with the garlic samosas.

NUTRITIONAL INFORMATION: Energy 658kcal/2744kJ; Protein 8.8g; Carbohydrate 63.4g, of which sugars 15.5g; Fat 42.8g, of which saturates 5.1g; Cholesterol 13mg Calcium 184mg; Fibre 5.9g; Sodium 375mg.

Thai Tofu Soup

This light, clear soup relies on an aromatic broth, mushrooms and tomatoes for its fine flavour.

ingredients

SERVES FOUR

- 115g/4oz/scant 2 cups dried shiitake mushrooms, soaked in water for 20 minutes
- 5ml/1 tsp sunflower oil
- 2 shallots, halved and sliced
- 2 chillies, seeded and sliced
- 4cm/1½in fresh root ginger, peeled and grated
- 350g/12oz tofu, rinsed, drained and cut into bitesize cubes
- 4 tomatoes, skinned, seeded and cut into thin strips
- salt and ground black pepper
- 1 bunch coriander (cilantro), stalks removed, finely chopped, to garnish

For the stock

- 4 celery sticks, sliced
- 4 carrots, sliced
- 1 small bulb of fennel, sliced
- 2 onions, peeled and quartered
- 6 tomatoes
- 2 garlic cloves, crushed
- 7.5cm/3in fresh root ginger, chopped
- 6 black peppercorns
- 2 star anise
- 4 cloves
- 1 cinnamon stick

1 Put all the stock ingredients in a large, heavy pan and pour in 2 litres/3½ pints/8 cups water. Bring to the boil, then reduce the heat and simmer gently with the lid on for 1½–2 hours.

2 Remove the lid and continue simmering for 30 minutes to reduce. Strain and measure out 1.5 litres/2½ pints/6¼ cups.

3 Squeeze the soaked shiitake mushrooms dry, remove the stems and slice the caps into thin strips.

4 Heat the oil in a large pan then stir in the shallots, chillies and ginger. Add the stock.

5 Add the tofu, mushrooms and tomatoes and bring to the boil. Reduce the heat and simmer gently for 5 minutes. Season and sprinkle with fresh coriander. Serve piping hot.

cook's tip

Dried and fresh shiitake mushrooms can be found in most Asian stores.

NUTRITIONAL INFORMATION: Energy 100kcal/418kJ; Protein 8.8g; Carbohydrate 5.2g, of which sugars 4.5g; Fat 5g, of which saturates 0.7g; Cholesterol 0mg; Calcium 430mg; Fibre 1.8g; Sodium 32mg.

Aubergine and Courgette Soup

A fusion of Greek flavours, this soup is served with a combination of cucumber and creamy yogurt.

ingredients

SERVES FOUR

- 2 large aubergines (eggplants), roughly diced
- 4 large courgettes (zucchini), roughly diced
- 1 onion, roughly chopped
- 4 garlic cloves, chopped
- 45ml/3 tbsp olive oil
- 1 2 litres/2 pints/5 cups vegetable stock
- 15ml/1 tbsp chopped fresh oregano
- salt and ground black pepper
- mint sprigs to garnish

For the tzatziki

- 1 cucumber, peeled, seeded and diced
- 10ml/2 tsp salt
- 225g/8oz/1 cup Greek (US strained plain) yogurt
- 2 garlic cloves, crushed
- 5ml/1 tsp white wine vinegar
- a little fresh mint, chopped

1 Preheat the oven to 200°C/400°F/Gas 6. Spread out the aubergines and courgettes in a roasting pan. Add the onion and garlic and drizzle with oil. Roast for 35 minutes, turning once, until the vegetables are tender and slightly charred.

2 For the tzatziki, place the cucumber in a colander. Sprinkle with the salt. Place on a bowl and leave for 30 minutes.

3 Pat the cucumber dry on kitchen paper and add to the yogurt with the garlic, vinegar, seasoning and chopped mint. Chill until required.

4 Place half the roasted vegetables in a food processor or blender. Add the stock and process until almost smooth. Then pour into a large heavy pan and add the remaining vegetables.

5 Bring the soup slowly to the boil and season well. Stir in the chopped oregano. Ladle the soup into four bowls. Garnish with mint sprigs and serve immediately. Hand round the bowl of tzatziki so that your guests can add a dollop or two to their soup as required.

cook's tip

Instead of using Greek yogurt in the tzatziki, try soured cream (sour cream) instead.

NUTRITIONAL INFORMATION: Energy 222kcal/920kJ; Protein 9.7g; Carbohydrate 12.7g, of which sugars 11g; Fat 15.7g, of which saturates 4.5g; Cholesterol 0mg; Calcium 192mg; Fibre 6.3g; Sodium 1034mg.

Mushroom and Bean Soup

This hearty Jewish soup is full of nutritious pulses and perfect on a freezing cold day.

ingredients

SERVES SIX TO EIGHT

- 30ml/2 tbsp small haricot (navy) beans, soaked overnight
- 45ml/ 3 tbsp green split peas
- 45ml/3 tbsp yellow split peas
- 90ml/6 tbsp pearl barley
- 1 onion, chopped
- 2 carrots, sliced
- 3 celery sticks, diced or sliced
- ½ baking potato, peeled and cut into chunks
- 10g/¼oz or 45ml/3 tbsp mixed dried mushrooms
- 5 garlic cloves, sliced
- 2 litres/3½ pints/8 cups water
- 2 vegetable stock (bouillon) cubes
- salt and ground black pepper
- 30–45ml/2–3 tbsp chopped fresh parsley, to garnish

3 Simmer gently for about 1½ hours, or until the beans and split peas are all tender.

1 In a pan, put the beans, split peas, pearl barley, onion, carrots, celery, potato, mushrooms, garlic and water.

2 Bring the mixture to the boil, then reduce the heat and cover the pan.

4 Crumble the stock cubes into the soup and taste for seasoning. Ladle into bowls, garnish with parsley and serve.

cook's tip

The mushrooms impart a rich flavour to this warming soup. Serve it with dark rye bread for a hearty meal.

NUTRITIONAL INFORMATION: Energy 171kcal/726kJ; Protein 7.7g; Carbohydrate 35.4g, of which sugars 3.7g; Fat 0.8g, of which saturates 0.1g; Cholesterol 0mg; Calcium 37mg; Fibre 3.3g; Sodium 27mg.

Spicy Chickpea Soup

Known as Harira, this Middle Eastern soup is often served in the evening during Ramadan.

ingredients

SERVES SIX

- 1 large onion
- 1 2 litres/2 pints/5 cups vegetable stock
- 5ml/1 tsp ground cinnamon
- 5ml/1 tsp turmeric
- 15ml/1 tbsp grated fresh root ginger
- pinch of cayenne pepper
- 2 carrots, diced
- 2 celery sticks, diced
- 400g/14oz can chopped tomatoes
- 450g/1 lb potatoes, diced
- 5 strands saffron
- 400g/14oz can chickpeas, drained
- 30ml/2 tbsp chopped fresh coriander (cilantro)
- 15ml/1 tbsp lemon juice
- salt and ground black pepper
- fried lemon wedges, to serve

1 Chop the onion finely and place in a large heavy pan with 300ml/¹/₂ pint/1¹/₄ cups of the vegetable stock. Bring the mixture slowly to the boil, then simmer gently for about 10 minutes. Remove from the heat.

2 Meanwhile, in a small bowl, mix together the cinnamon, turmeric, ginger, cayenne pepper and 30ml/2 tbsp of the stock to form a paste. Stir the paste into the onion mixture with the carrots, the celery and the remaining stock.

3 Bring the mixture to the boil, reduce the heat, then cover and simmer gently for 5 minutes.

4 Add the tomatoes and potatoes and simmer gently, covered, for 20 minutes. Add the saffron, chickpeas, coriander and lemon juice. Season, and serve piping hot with fried wedges of lemon.

NUTRITIONAL INFORMATION: Energy 158kcal/668kJ; Protein 7.2g; Carbohydrate 28.4g, of which sugars 7g; Fat 2.5g, of which saturates 0.4g; Cholesterol 0mg; Calcium 64mg; Fibre 5.4g; Sodium 173mg.

Baked Bean and Pistou Soup

This vegetarian soup has a mixed bean base and is flavoured with a basil and cheese sauce.

ingredients

SERVES FOUR TO SIX

- 150g/5oz/scant 1 cup dried haricot (navy) beans, soaked overnight in cold water
- 150g/5oz/scant 1 cup dried flageolet or cannellini beans, soaked overnight in cold water
- 1 onion, chopped
- 1.2 litres/2 pints/5 cups hot vegetable stock
- 2 carrots, roughly chopped
- 225g/8oz Savoy cabbage, shredded
- 1 large potato, roughly chopped
- 225g/8oz green beans, chopped
- salt and ground black pepper
- basil leaves, to garnish

For the pistou
- 4 garlic cloves
- 8 large basil sprigs
- 90ml/6 tbsp olive oil
- 60ml/4 tbsp freshly grated Parmesan cheese

1 Drain the haricot and flageolet or cannellini beans. Place in a large casserole. Add the onion and cold water to cover the beans by 5cm/2in. Cover and place in the oven. Set the oven at 200°C/400°F/Gas 6 and cook for 1¹/₂ hours, until the beans are tender. Reduce the oven temperature to 180°C/350°F/Gas 4.

2 Drain the beans and onions, and purée half the mixture in a food processor or blender. Return the whole beans and purée to the casserole.

3 Add the hot vegetable stock, carrots, cabbage, potato and green beans. Season, cover and replace in the oven. Cook for 1 hour or until all the vegetables are tender.

4 Make the pistou: place the garlic and basil in a mortar and pound with a pestle, then gradually beat in the oil. Stir in the grated Parmesan.

5 Stir half the pistou into the soup and serve each bowl with a spoonful of the remaining pistou garnished with basil.

cook's tip

Boil dried beans in unsalted water. Salt toughens them if it is added before they are completely cooked.

NUTRITIONAL INFORMATION: Energy 338kcal/1416kJ; Protein 17.2g; Carbohydrate 34.6g, of which sugars 7.5g; Fat 15.5g, of which saturates 3.8g; Cholesterol 10mg; Calcium 215mg; Fibre 10.8g; Sodium 133mg.

Spiced Black-eyed Bean Broth

Here, black-eyed beans are delicious in a turmeric-tinted tomato broth flavoured with tangy lemon.

ingredients

SERVES FOUR

- 175g/6oz/1 cup dried black-eyed beans (peas)
- 15ml/1 tbsp olive oil
- 2 onions, chopped
- 4 garlic cloves, chopped
- 1 medium-hot or 2–3 mild fresh chillies, chopped
- 5ml/1 tsp ground cumin
- 5ml/1 tsp ground turmeric
- 250g/9oz fresh or canned tomatoes, diced
- 600ml/1 pint/2½ cups chicken, beef or vegetable stock
- 25g/1oz fresh coriander (cilantro) leaves, roughly chopped
- juice of ½ lemon
- pitta bread, to serve

1 Put the beans in a pan, cover with water, bring to the boil, then cook for 5 minutes. Remove from the heat.

2 Cover the beans and leave to stand for 2 hours. Drain through a sieve (strainer) and discard the cooking liquid, return the beans to the rinsed-out pan, cover with fresh cold water, then bring them to the boil. Reduce the heat to low and cover and simmer for 35–40 minutes, or until the beans are tender. Drain well then set the beans aside.

3 Heat the oil in a pan, add the onions, garlic and chilli and cook for 5 minutes. Stir in the cumin, turmeric, tomatoes, stock, half the coriander and the beans and bring to the boil. Reduce the heat, cover the pan and simmer for 20–30 minutes.

4 Stir the lemon juice and remaining chopped coriander leaves into the soup and serve immediately with pitta bread.

cook's tip

Buy dried beans from a store that has a good turnover, and check the sell-by dates. Beans that are old take a long time to cook and tenderize.

NUTRITIONAL INFORMATION: Energy 172kcal/727kJ; Protein 10.9g; Carbohydrate 25.4g, of which sugars 6g; Fat 3.7g, of which saturates 0.6g; Cholesterol 0mg; Calcium 73mg; Fibre 8.5g; Sodium 17mg.

Borlotti Bean Soup with Pasta

A complete meal in a bowl, this is an inspired version of a classic Italian soup.

ingredients

SERVES FOUR

- 1 onion, chopped
- 1 celery stick, chopped
- 2 carrots, chopped
- 75ml/5 tbsp olive oil
- 1 bay leaf
- 1 glass white wine (optional)
- 1 litre/1¾ pints/4 cups vegetable stock
- 400g/14oz can chopped tomatoes
- 300ml/½ pint/1¼ cups passata (bottled strained tomatoes)
- 175g/6oz/1½ cups pasta shapes, such as farfalle or conchiglie
- 400g/14oz can borlotti beans, drained
- 250g/9oz spinach
- salt and ground black pepper
- 50g/2oz/⅔ cup freshly grated Parmesan cheese, to serve

1 Place the onion, celery and carrots in a large pan with the olive oil. Cook over a medium heat for 5 minutes.

2 Add the bay leaf, wine, if using, stock, tomatoes and passata.

3 Bring to the boil. Lower the heat and simmer for 10 minutes until the vegetables are tender.

4 Add the pasta and beans, and bring the soup back to the boil, then simmer for 8 minutes until the pasta is *al dente*. Stir often.

5 Season to taste with salt and ground black pepper. Remove any thick stalks from the spinach and add the leaves to the soup. Cook the soup for a further 2 minutes. Serve in four heated bowls and sprinkle each with freshly grated Parmesan cheese.

NUTRITIONAL INFORMATION: Energy 321kcal/1363kJ; Protein 15g; Carbohydrate 57.8g, of which sugars 12.7g; Fat 5g, of which saturates 0.8g; Cholesterol 0mg; Calcium 166mg; Fibre 9.9g; Sodium 762mg.

Pasta, Bean and Vegetable Soup

This rustic Italian speciality can be made with a huge range of ingredients.

ingredients

SERVES FOUR TO SIX

- 75g/3oz/scant ½ cup brown lentils
- 15g/½oz dried mushrooms
- 60ml/4 tbsp olive oil
- 1 carrot, diced
- 1 celery stick, diced
- 1 onion, finely chopped
- 1 garlic clove, finely chopped
- a little chopped fresh flat leaf parsley
- a good pinch of crushed red chillies (optional)
- 1.5 litres/2½ pints/6¼ cups vegetable stock
- 150g/5oz/scant 1 cup each canned red kidney beans, cannellini beans and chickpeas, rinsed and drained
- 115g/4oz/1 cup dried small pasta shapes, such as rigatoni, penne or penne rigate
- salt and ground black pepper
- chopped flat leaf parsley, to garnish
- freshly grated Pecorino cheese, to serve

1 Put the lentils in a medium pan, add 475ml/16fl oz/2 cups water and bring to the boil over a high heat. Lower the heat to a gentle simmer and cook, stirring occasionally, for 15–20 minutes or until the lentils are just tender. Meanwhile, soak the dried mushrooms in 175ml/6fl oz/³⁄₄ cup warm water for 15–20 minutes.

2 Strain the lentils, then rinse. Drain the soaked mushrooms and reserve the soaking liquid. Finely chop the mushrooms and set aside.

3 Heat the oil in a large pan and add the carrot, celery, onion, garlic, parsley and chillies, if using. Cook over a low heat for 5–7 minutes, until the vegetables are soft.

4 Add the stock, the mushrooms and their soaking liquid. Bring to the boil, then add the beans, chickpeas and lentils. Return to the boil, cover and simmer for 20 minutes.

5 Add the pasta and bring back to the boil, stirring constantly. Simmer for 7–8 minutes, until the pasta is *al dente*. Season to taste, then divide the soup among warmed bowls, garnish with parsley and serve with grated Pecorino.

NUTRITIONAL INFORMATION: Energy 668kcal/2831kJ; Protein 41.4g; Carbohydrate 100.8g, of which sugars 7.5g; Fat 14g, of which saturates 2g; Cholesterol 0mg; Calcium 178mg; Fibre 26.1g; Sodium 44mg.

Roasted Tomato and Pasta Soup

Roasting concentrates the flavour of tomatoes and this soup has a wonderful, smoky taste.

ingredients

SERVES FOUR

- 450g/1lb ripe plum tomatoes, halved lengthways
- 1 large red (bell) pepper, quartered lengthways and seeded
- 1 large red onion, quartered lengthways
- 2 garlic cloves, unpeeled
- 15ml/1 tbsp olive oil
- 1.2 litres/2 pints/5 cups vegetable stock or water
- a good pinch of sugar
- 90g/3½oz/scant 1 cup small pasta shapes, such as tubetti or small macaroni
- salt and ground black pepper
- fresh basil leaves, to garnish

1 Preheat the oven to 190°C/375°F/Gas 5. Spread out the tomatoes, red pepper, onion and garlic in a roasting pan and drizzle with the olive oil. Roast for 30–40 minutes until the vegetables are soft and charred, stirring and turning them halfway through cooking.

cook's tip

You can roast the vegetables in advance, allow them to cool, then leave them in a covered bowl until needed.

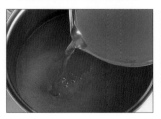

2 Transfer the vegetables into a food processor or blender, add about 250ml/8fl oz/1 cup of the stock or water, and process until puréed. Scrape into a sieve (strainer) placed over a large pan and press the purée through into the pan.

3 Add the remaining stock or water, the sugar and season to taste. Bring to the boil.

4 Add the pasta and simmer for 7–8 minutes (or according to the instructions on the packet). Stir frequently, and check that the pasta is *al dente*, that is, tender but not flabby, with a bit of bite. Taste and adjust the seasoning if necessary with salt and freshly ground black pepper. Serve hot in four warmed bowls, garnished with the fresh basil leaves.

NUTRITIONAL INFORMATION: Energy 128kcal/543kJ; Protein 4.5g; Carbohydrate 26.9g, of which sugars 9.7g; Fat 1g, of which saturates 0.2g; Cholesterol 0mg; Calcium 30mg; Fibre 3.2g; Sodium 14mg.

Egg and Lemon Soup with Pasta

Egg and lemon mixed together and then cooled to make a creamy soup is a Mediterranean favourite.

ingredients

SERVES FOUR TO SIX

• 1.75 litres/3 pints/7½ cups chicken stock
• 115g/4oz/½ cup orzo pasta
• 3 eggs
• juice of 1 large lemon
• salt and ground black pepper
• lemon slices, to garnish

cook's tip

· Do not let the soup boil once the eggs have been added or it will curdle. Take care when using a heavy-bottomed pan that retains heat because the soup may continue to simmer for some time after the heat has been reduced and this also can cause curdling.

· This version uses tiny orzo pasta to make a heartier dish than the classic avgolemono.

variations

Replace orzo with other small pasta such as stellette (stars) or orecchiette (little ears). The cooking times should be the same. Instead of chicken stock, use vegetable stock.

1 Pour the stock into a large pan, and bring it to the boil. Add the pasta and cook for a further 5 minutes, until *al dente*.

2 Beat the eggs with a fork until they are frothy, then add the lemon juice and a tablespoon of cold water. Slowly stir in a ladleful of the hot chicken stock, then add one or two more.

3 Reduce the heat under the pan to the lowest setting. Add the egg mixture to the soup in the pan, stirring all the time. Immediately remove the pan from the heat and stir well.

4 Season with salt and ground black pepper and serve immediately, garnished with lemon slices.

NUTRITIONAL INFORMATION: Energy 104kcal/438kJ; Protein 5.5g; Carbohydrate 14.3g, of which sugars 0.7g; Fat 3.2g, of which saturates 0.8g; Cholesterol 95mg; Calcium 20mg; Fibre 0.6g; Sodium 117mg.

Summer Minestrone

This classic Italian soup is made lighter and fresher with the addition of young vegetables.

ingredients

SERVES SIX

- 2 onions, finely chopped
- 2 garlic cloves, finely chopped
- 30ml/2 tbsp olive oil
- 2 carrots, very finely chopped
- 1 celery stick, very finely chopped
- 1.27 litres/2¼ pints/5⅔ cups boiling water
- 450g/1lb shelled fresh broad (fava) beans
- 225g/8oz mangetouts (snow peas), cut into fine strips
- 3 tomatoes, peeled and chopped
- 5ml/1 tsp tomato purée (paste)
- 50g/2oz spaghettini, broken into 4cm/1½in lengths
- 225g/8oz baby spinach
- 30ml/2 tbsp chopped fresh parsley
- handful of fresh basil leaves
- salt and ground black pepper
- basil sprigs, to garnish
- freshly grated Parmesan cheese, to serve

1 Cook the onions and garlic in the oil for 4–5 minutes. Add the carrots and celery. Cook for 2–3 minutes. Add the water and simmer for 15 minutes, until the vegetables are tender.

2 Cook the beans in boiling water for 4–5 minutes. Remove with a slotted spoon, refresh under cold water and set aside.

3 Bring the pan of water back to the boil, add the mangetouts and cook for 1 minute until tender. Drain, refresh and set aside.

4 Add the tomatoes and the tomato purée to the soup. Cook for 1 minute. Purée two or three large ladlefuls of the soup and a quarter of the broad beans in a food processor or blender until smooth. Set aside.

5 Add the spaghettini to the remaining soup and cook for 6–8 minutes, until tender. Stir in the purée and the spinach and cook for 2–3 minutes. Add the rest of the broad beans, the mangetouts and the parsley, and season well with salt and freshly ground black pepper.

6 Stir in the basil leaves and ladle the soup into six bowls. Garnish with sprigs of basil. Serve immediately, with a little grated Parmesan.

NUTRITIONAL INFORMATION: Energy 201kcal/839kJ; Protein 8.1g; Carbohydrate 18.1g, of which sugars 7.8g; Fat 11.2g, of which saturates 3.4g; Cholesterol 110mg; Calcium 170mg; Fibre 3g; Sodium 138mg.

Pasta and Red Pepper in Broth

This simple soup makes a delicious first course for an al fresco supper served with ciabatta bread.

ingredients

SERVES FOUR

- 1.2 litres/2 pints/5 cups well-flavoured vegetable or chicken stock
- 75g/3oz/¾ cup tiny soup pasta
- 2 pieces bottled roasted red (bell) pepper, about 50g/2oz
- coarsely shaved Parmesan cheese, to serve

cook's tip

Soup pasta is called pastini in Italian and is now widely available. Choose one shape or colour, or use a mixture for an interesting result. There are many different pastini to choose from, including stellette (stars), anellini (tiny thin rounds), risoni (rice-shaped) and farfalline (little butterflies). You could also use the fine "angel hair" pasta, capellini, broken into smaller pieces.

for 7–8 minutes, until the pasta shapes are *al dente*, or tender but still firm to the bite. Drain the pasta through a sieve.

1 Bring the stock to the boil in a large pan. Add seasoning to taste, then drop in the dried soup pasta. Stir well and bring the stock back to the boil.

2 Reduce the heat so that the soup simmers gently and cook

3 Drain the pepper, dry with kitchen paper and dice. Divide it among four warmed soup plates.

4 Taste the soup and adjust the seasoning if necessary. Ladle it on top of the diced pepper in the four warmed soup plates. Serve the soup topped with a few shavings of Parmesan cheese.

NUTRITIONAL INFORMATION: Energy 79kcal/334kJ; Protein 2.9g; Carbohydrate 15.9g, of which sugars 2.4g; Fat 0.8g, of which saturates 0.1g; Cholesterol 0mg; Calcium 13mg; Fibre 1g; Sodium 426mg.

Cappelletti in Broth

Cappelletti are stuffed pasta shapes, usually filled with meat, which are said to resemble hats.

ingredients

SERVES FOUR

- 1.2 litres/2 pints/5 cups home-made chicken stock
- 90g/3½oz/1 cup fresh or dried cappelletti
- 30ml/2 tbsp dry white wine
- about 45ml/3 tbsp finely chopped fresh flat leaf parsley (optional)
- about 30ml/2 tbsp freshly grated Parmesan cheese
- salt and ground black pepper

variation

Use other small filled pasta shapes such as tortellini or, for a light soup, use soup pasta.

1 Pour the chicken stock into a large pan and bring to the boil. Season to taste, then drop in the pasta.

2 Stir the pasta well and bring back to the boil. Lower the heat to just above a simmer and

cook until the pasta is *al dente*, or tender but still with a bit of a bite.

3 Swirl in the wine and parsley, if using, then taste and adjust the seasoning with salt and ground black pepper.

4 Ladle into four warmed soup plates, then sprinkle generously with the freshly grated Parmesan cheese and serve immediately.

cook's tip

This soup needs a well-flavoured stock as a base. If you don't have home-made stock use two 300g/11oz cans of condensed beef consommé, adding water as instructed, or buy good quality chilled commercial chicken stock.

NUTRITIONAL INFORMATION: Energy 111kcal/469kJ; Protein 5.8g; Carbohydrate 16.7g, of which sugars 0.8g; Fat 3g, of which saturates 1.6g; Cholesterol 8mg; Calcium 96mg; Fibre 0.7g; Sodium 228mg.

Pasta and Brown Lentil Soup

This rustic vegetarian soup makes a hearty and warming winter meal with crusty Italian bread.

ingredients

SERVES FOUR TO SIX

- 75g/6oz/¾ cup brown lentils
- 3 garlic cloves, unpeeled
- litre/1¾ pints/4 cups boiling water
- 15ml/3 tbsp olive oil
- 25g,1oz/2 tbsp butter
- onion, finely chopped
- 2 celery sticks, finely chopped
- 30ml/2 tbsp sun-dried tomato paste
- .75 litres/3 pints/7½ cups vegetable stock
- few fresh marjoram leaves
- few fresh basil leaves
- leaves from 1 fresh thyme sprig
- 50g/2oz/½ cup small pasta shapes, such as macaroni or tubeti
- salt and ground black pepper
- tiny fresh herb leaves, such as thyme or marjoram, to garnish

1 Put the lentils in a large pan. Smash one of the garlic cloves using the blade of a large knife (there is no need to peel it first), then add it to the lentils. Pour in the boiling water and bring the lentils back to the boil. Reduce the heat, partly cover and simmer the lentils for about 20 minutes, or until they are tender.

2 Drain the lentils in a sieve (strainer), remove the garlic and set it aside. Rinse the lentils under the cold tap and leave to drain.

3 Heat 30ml/2 tbsp of the oil with half the butter in the pan. Add the onion and celery and cook gently for 5 minutes.

4 Crush the remaining garlic, then peel and mash the reserved garlic. Add to the pan with the remaining oil, the tomato paste and the lentils. Add the stock, marjoram, basil, thyme and salt and ground black pepper.

5 Bring to the boil and simmer for 30 minutes. Add the pasta and bring the soup back to the boil, stirring. Reduce the heat and simmer until the pasta is just tender. Stir in the remaining butter.

6 Season, then serve in four to six warmed bowls, sprinkled with fresh herb leaves such as thyme or marjoram to garnish.

NUTRITIONAL INFORMATION: Energy 179kcal/753kJ; Protein 8.4g; Carbohydrate 24.2g, of which sugars 2.3g; Fat 6.1g, of which saturates 0.9g; Cholesterol 26mg; Calcium 25mg; Fibre 2.1g; Sodium 29mg.

Chicken Noodle Soup

This is a really traditional chicken noodle soup – clear, golden and warming.

ingredients

SERVES FOUR TO SIX

- 2kg/4½lb boiling fowl (stewing chicken) with the giblets (except the liver)
- 1 large onion, peeled and halved
- 2 large carrots, halved lengthways
- 6 celery sticks, roughly chopped
- 1 bay leaf
- 175g/6oz vermicelli pasta
- whole parsley leaves
- salt and ground black pepper

1 Put the chicken into a large pan with all the vegetables and the bay leaf. Cover with 2.4 litres/4 pints/10 cups cold water. Bring slowly to the boil, carefully skimming off any scum that rises to the top. Add salt and pepper.

2 Turn down the heat and simmer the soup slowly for at least 2 hours, or until the fowl is tender and the meat falls off the bones. When the soup is simmering, the surface of the liquid should just tremble. If it is allowed to boil, the soup will become cloudy.

3 When the chicken is tender, remove the bird and strip the flesh off the carcass. (Use the meat in sandwiches or in a risotto.) Return the bones to the soup and simmer for another hour.

4 Strain the soup into a bowl, cool, then chill overnight. The next day the soup should have set to a solid jelly and will be covered with a thin layer of solidified chicken fat. Carefully remove the fat by gently scraping it off with a knife.

5 To serve the soup, reheat in a large pan. Add the vermicelli and parsley leaves, and simmer for 6–8 minutes until the pasta is cooked. Taste and adjust the seasoning. Serve piping hot in four to six warmed soup bowls.

NUTRITIONAL INFORMATION: Energy 176kcal/748kJ; Protein 6.3g; Carbohydrate 37.5g, of which sugars 5.7g; Fat 1.2g, of which saturates 0.1g; Cholesterol 0mg; Calcium 66mg; Fibre 3.4g; Sodium 39mg.

Chiang Mai Noodle Soup

This soup is full of flavourful ingredients that are given an added kick from fiery chillies.

ingredients

SERVES FOUR TO SIX

- 600ml/1 pint/2½ cups coconut milk
- 30ml/2 tbsp Thai red curry paste
- 5ml/1 tsp ground turmeric
- 450g/1lb chicken thighs, boned and cut into bitesize chunks
- 600ml/1 pint/2½ cups chicken stock
- 60ml/4 tbsp Thai fish sauce
- 15ml/1 tbsp dark soy sauce
- juice of ½–1 lime
- 450g/1lb fresh egg noodles, blanched in boiling water
- salt and ground black pepper

To garnish

- 3 spring onions (scallions), chopped
- 4 fresh red chillies, chopped
- 4 shallots, chopped
- 60ml/4 tbsp sliced pickled mustard leaves (optional)
- 30ml/2 tbsp fried sliced garlic
- 15ml/1 tbsp chopped fresh coriander (cilantro) leaves

1 Pour about one-third of the coconut milk into a large, heavy pan or wok. Slowly bring to the boil over a medium heat, stirring often until the milk separates.

2 Add the curry paste and ground turmeric, stir to mix completely and cook until the mixture is fragrant.

3 Add the chicken and toss over the heat for about 2 minutes, making sure that all the chunks are thoroughly coated with the paste.

4 Add the remaining coconut milk, the chicken stock, fish sauce and soy sauce. Season to taste. Bring to simmering point, stirring often, then lower the heat and cook gently for 7–10 minutes, until the chicken is cooked. Remove from the heat and stir in lime juice to taste.

5 Reheat the egg noodles in boiling water, drain and divide among four to six warmed bowls. Divide the chicken among the bowls and ladle in the hot soup. Top each serving with spring onions, chopped red chillies, shallots, mustard leaves, if using, garlic, and coriander leaves. Serve the soup immediately.

NUTRITIONAL INFORMATION: Energy 679kcal/2873kJ; Protein 43.2g; Carbohydrate 88.7g, of which sugars 10.1g; Fat 19.4g, of which saturates 5.6g; Cholesterol 180mg; Calcium 95mg; Fibre 3.4g; Sodium 769mg.

Cellophane Noodle Soup

The noodles used in this soup go by various names: glass, cellophane, bean thread or transparent.

ingredients

SERVES FOUR

- 4 dried shiitake mushrooms
- 15g/½oz dried lily buds (optional)
- ½ cucumber, chopped
- 2 garlic cloves, halved
- 90g/3½oz white cabbage, coarsely chopped
- 1.2 litres/2 pints/5 cups boiling water
- 115g/4oz cellophane noodles
- 30ml/2 tbsp soy sauce
- 15ml/1 tbsp light muscovado (brown) sugar
- 90g/3½oz silken tofu, diced
- fresh coriander (cilantro) leaves, to garnish

1 Soak the shiitake mushrooms in warm water for 30 minutes. In a separate bowl, soak the dried lily buds, if using, in warm water, also for 30 minutes.

2 Meanwhile, put the chopped cucumber, garlic and cabbage in a food processor or blender and process to a smooth paste. Scrape the mixture

into a large pan and add the measured boiling water. Bring to the boil. Reduce the heat and cook for 2 minutes, stirring occasionally.

3 Strain the stock into another pan, return to a low heat and bring to simmering point.

4 Drain the lily buds, rinse under cold running water, then drain again. Cut off any hard ends. Add the lily buds to the stock with the noodles, soy sauce and sugar and cook for 5 minutes more.

5 Strain the mushroom soaking liquid into the soup. Discard the mushroom stems, then slice the caps thinly. Divide the caps and the tofu among four bowls. Divide the soup among the bowls, garnish with coriander and serve.

cook's tip

Dried lily flowers are available at Chinese supermarkets.

NUTRITIONAL INFORMATION: Energy 148kcal/618kJ; Protein 4.1g; Carbohydrate 29.7g, of which sugars 5.7g; Fat 1.1g, of which saturates 0.1g; Cholesterol 0mg; Calcium 139mg; Fibre 0.7g; Sodium 546mg.

Red Onion Laksa

Sliced red onions mimic flour noodles in this soup

ingredients

SERVES SIX

- 150g/5oz/2½ cups dried shiitake mushrooms
- 1.2 litres/2 pints/5 cups boiling vegetable stock
- 30ml/2 tbsp tamarind paste
- 250ml/8fl oz/1 cup boiling water
- 6 large dried red chillies, stems removed and seeded
- 2 lemon grass stalks, finely sliced
- 5ml/1 tsp ground turmeric
- 15ml/1 tbsp grated fresh galangal or fresh root ginger
- 1 onion, chopped
- 5ml/1 tsp dried shrimp paste
- 30ml/2 tbsp vegetable oil
- 10ml/2 tsp palm sugar (jaggery)
- 175g/6oz rice vermicelli
- 1 red onion, very finely sliced
- 1 small cucumber, seeded and cut into strips
- handful of fresh mint sprigs, to garnish

1 Place the mushrooms in a bowl and pour in enough boiling stock to cover them, then leave to soak for 30 minutes. Put the tamarind paste into a bowl and pour in half the boiling water. Mash, strain and reserve the liquid, discarding the pulp.

2 Soak the chillies in the remaining boiling water for 5 minutes, then drain, reserving the liquid. Place in a food processor or blender and blend with the lemon grass, turmeric, galangal or ginger, onion and shrimp paste.

3 Heat the oil and cook the paste for 4–5 minutes. Add the tamarind liquid and bring to the boil. Simmer for 5 minutes, then remove from the heat.

4 Drain the mushrooms and reserve the stock. Discard the stems, then halve the caps. Add to the pan with their soaking liquid, the remaining stock and the sugar. Simmer for 25–30 minutes.

5 Put the rice vermicelli into a large bowl and cover with boiling water, then leave to soak for 4 minutes. Drain well, then divide among six bowls. Top each bowl with onion and cucumber, then ladle in the shiitake soup. Add a few mint sprigs to each bowl and serve.

NUTRITIONAL INFORMATION: Energy 161kcal/671kJ; Protein 4.1g; Carbohydrate 26.6g, of which sugars 2.7g; Fat 4.3g, of which saturates 0.6g; Cholesterol 4mg; Calcium 32mg; Fibre 0.2g; Sodium 41mg.

Japanese-style Noodle Soup

This delicate, fragrant soup is flavoured with a subtle hint of chilli. It makes a delicious light lunch.

ingredients

SERVES FOUR

- 45ml/3 tbsp mugi miso
- 200g/7oz/scant 2 cups udon noodles, soba noodles or Chinese noodles
- 30ml/2 tbsp sake or dry sherry
- 15ml/1 tbsp rice or wine vinegar
- 45ml/3 tbsp Japanese soy sauce
- 115g/4oz asparagus tips or mangetours (snow peas), thinly sliced diagonally
- 50g/2oz/scant 1 cup shiitake mushrooms, stalks removed and thinly sliced
- 1 carrot, sliced into strips
- 3 spring onions (scallions), thinly sliced diagonally
- salt and ground black pepper
- 5ml/1 tsp dried chilli flakes, to serve

1 Bring 1 litre/1³/₄ pints/ 4 cups water to the boil in a pan. Pour 150ml/¹/₄ pint/ ²/₃ cup boiling water over the miso and stir until dissolved, then set aside.

2 Meanwhile, bring another large pan of lightly salted water to the boil, add the noodles and cook until just tender.

3 Drain the noodles in a colander. Rinse under cold running water, then drain again. Set aside.

4 Add the sake or sherry, rice or wine vinegar and soy sauce to the boiling water. Boil gently for 3 minutes or until the alcohol has evaporated, then reduce the heat and stir in the miso mixture.

5 Add the asparagus or mangetouts, mushrooms, carrot and spring onions, and simmer for 2 minutes until the vegetables are tender. Season to taste.

6 Divide the noodles among four bowls. Add the soup, then the chilli flakes.

NUTRITIONAL INFORMATION: Energy 365kcal/1522kJ; Protein 12.5g; Carbohydrate 54.1g, of which sugars 3.9g; Fat 10.9g, of which saturates 3.9g; Cholesterol 0mg; Calcium 43mg; Fibre 1.7g; Sodium 569mg.

Noodle Soup with Tofu

This light and refreshing soup is an excellent pick-me-up with an aromatic, spicy broth.

ingredients

SERVES FOUR

- 150g/5oz dried thick rice noodles
- 1 litre/1¾ pints/4 cups vegetable stock
- 1 fresh red chilli, seeded and thinly sliced
- 15ml/1 tbsp light soy sauce
- juice of ½ lemon
- 10ml/2 tsp sugar
- 5ml/1 tsp finely sliced garlic
- 5ml/1 tsp finely chopped fresh root ginger
- 200g/7oz firm tofu
- 90g/3½oz/scant 1 cup beansprouts
- 50g/2oz/½ cup peanuts
- 15ml/1 tbsp chopped fresh coriander (cilantro)

For the garnish

- spring onion (scallion) slivers
- red chilli slivers

1 Spread out the noodles in a shallow dish and cover with boiling water. Soak according to the packet instructions, until they are just tender. Drain, rinse and set aside.

2 Meanwhile, place the stock, red chilli, soy sauce, lemon juice, sugar, garlic and ginger in

a pan over a high heat. Bring to the boil, cover, reduce to a low heat and simmer the mixture gently for 10–12 minutes.

3 With a sharp knife, cut the tofu into cubes. Add it to the soup with the drained noodles

and the beansprouts. Cook the mixture gently for a further 2–3 minutes.

4 Roast the peanuts in a wok or frying pan, then chop them. Stir the coriander into the soup. Serve the soup ladled into warm bowls with peanuts, spring on ons and chilli scattered over the top.

cook's tip

It is important to use vegetable stock with plenty of flavour for this simple soup.

NUTRITIONAL INFORMATION: Energy 261kcal/1092kJ; Protein 10g; Carbohydrate 36.4g, of which sugars 4.3g; Fat 8g, of which saturates 1.4g; Cholesterol 0mg; Calcium 275mg; Fibre 1.2g; Sodium 97mg.

Spiced Squash Noodle Soup

This full-flavoured soup, or chorba, is the daily dish in many Moroccan households.

ingredients

SERVES FOUR

- 1 butternut squash
- 8 large, ripe tomatoes
- 45ml/3 tbsp olive oil
- 3–4 whole cloves
- 2 onions, chopped
- 4 celery sticks, chopped
- 2 carrots, chopped
- 5ml/1 tsp sugar
- 15ml/1 tbsp tomato purée (paste)
- 5–10ml/1–2 tsp ras el hanout
- 2.5ml/½ tsp ground turmeric
- a large bunch of fresh coriander (cilantro), chopped
- 1.75 litres/3 pints/7½ cups vegetable stock
- handful of dried egg noodles or cappellini, broken into pieces
- salt and ground black pepper
- natural (plain) yogurt and coriander (cilantro), to garnish

1 Halve the squash, remove the seeds and peel, then cut the flesh into small chunks. Peel and chop the tomatoes.

2 In a deep, heavy pan, heat the oil and add the cloves, onions, squash, celery and carrots. Fry until the vegetables begin to colour, then stir in the chopped tomatoes and sugar. Cook, stirring, until the liquid reduces and the tomatoes pulp.

3 Stir in the tomato purée, the ras el hanout, the turmeric and the chopped coriander. Pour in

the vegetable stock and bring to the boil. Reduce the heat and simmer, uncovered, for 30–40 minutes until the vegetables are soft and the liquid is reduced a little.

4 To make a smooth soup, let the soup cool slightly before processing it in a food processor or blender, then pour it back into the pan.

5 Add the noodles or pasta to the soup and simmer for 10 minutes, until it is *al dente* or just tender. Ladle the

soup into bowls and serve topped with the yogurt and coriander.

variation

For extra flavour, add a crushed garlic clove and salt to the yogurt.

NUTRITIONAL INFORMATION: Energy 265kcal/1108kJ; Protein 6.9g; Carbohydrate 37.8g, of which sugars 20.2g; Fat 10.2g, of which saturates 1.7g; Cholesterol 0mg; Calcium 158mg; Fibre 8.1g; Sodium 64mg.

Noodle and Vegetable Soup

This simple soup is fun to make and tasty to eat, and is popular with children.

ingredients

SERVES FOUR

- 1 yellow (bell) pepper
- 2 large courgettes (zucchini)
- 2 large carrots
- 1 kohlrabi
- 900ml/1½ pints/3¾ cups well-flavoured vegetable stock
- 50g/2oz rice vermicelli
- salt and ground black pepper

1 Cut the yellow pepper into quarters, removing the stalk, seeds and the core. Cut the courgettes and carrots lengthways into 5 mm/¼in thick slices and slice the kohlrabi into rounds about 5 mm/¼in thick.

2 Using tiny pastry cutters, stamp out different shapes from the vegetables or use a very sharp knife to cut the sliced vegetables into free-form stars and other decorative shapes. You can be as creative with this as you like.

3 Place the vegetables and stock in a pan and simmer for 10 minutes, until the vegetables are tender. Season to taste with salt and pepper.

4 Meanwhile, place the vermicelli in a large bowl, cover with boiling water and set aside for 4 minutes. Drain well, then divide the vermicelli among four soup bowls. Ladle the soup into the bowls and serve.

NUTRITIONAL INFORMATION: Energy 120kcal/501kJ; Protein 4.1g; Carbohydrate 24.3g, of which sugars 13.6g; Fat 1g, of which saturates 0.3g; Cholesterol 0mg; Calcium 63mg; Fibre 4.6g; Sodium 526mg.

Chicken and Leek Soup

This recipe is based on the traditional Scottish Cock-a-leekie. The inclusion of prunes is delicious.

ingredients

SERVES SIX

- 1 chicken, weighing about 2kg/4¼lb
- 900g/2lb leeks
- 1 fresh bay leaf
- a few each fresh parsley stalks and thyme sprigs
- 1 large carrot, thickly sliced
- 2.4 litres/4 pints/10 cups chicken or beef stock
- 115g/4oz/generous ½ cup pearl barley
- 400g/14oz prunes
- salt and ground black pepper
- chopped fresh parsley, to garnish

1 Cut the breasts off the chicken and set aside. Place the remaining carcass in a large pan. Cut half the leeks into 5cm/2in lengths and add them to the pan. Tie the bay leaf, parsley and thyme into a bouquet garni and add with the carrot and the stock. Bring to the boil, then reduce the heat, cover and simmer for 1 hour. Skim off any scum.

2 Add the chicken breasts and cook for another 30 minutes, until they are just cooked. Leave until cool enough to handle,

then strain the stock. Reserve the chicken breasts and the meat from the chicken carcass. Discard all the skin, bones, cooked vegetables and herbs. Skim as much fat as you can from the stock, then return it to the pan.

3 Meanwhile, rinse the pearl barley thoroughly in a sieve (strainer) under cold running water, then add it to a large pan of boiling water. Bring to the boil then simmer for about 10 minutes. Drain, rinse well again and drain thoroughly.

4 Add the pearl barley to the stock. Bring to the boil then lower the heat and cook gently for 15–20 minutes.

5 Add the prunes. Slice the remaining leeks and add them to the pan. Bring to the boil, then simmer for 10 minutes.

6 Slice the chicken breasts and add them to the soup with the remaining chicken meat, sliced into neat pieces. Reheat and season, then ladle the soup into deep plates and sprinkle with parsley.

NUTRITIONAL INFORMATION: Energy 359kcal/1526kJ; Protein 41.7g; Carbohydrate 44g, of which sugars 26.9g; Fat 3g, of which saturates 0.6g; Cholesterol 105mg; Calcium 73mg; Fibre 7.4g; Sodium 104mg.

Chicken, Corn and Bean Soup

Based on a vegetable dish from the southern USA, this soup includes succulent fresh corn kernels.

ingredients

SERVES FOUR

- 750ml/1¼ pints/3 cups chicken stock
- 4 boneless, skinless chicken breasts
- 50g/2oz/¼ cup butter
- 2 onions, chopped
- 115g/4oz piece rindless smoked streaky (fatty) bacon, chopped
- 25g/1oz/¼ cup plain (all-purpose) flour
- corn kernels from 4 cobs of corn
- 300ml/½ pint/1¼ cups milk
- 400g/14oz can butter (lima) beans, drained
- 45ml/3 tbsp chopped fresh parsley
- salt and ground black pepper

1 Bring the chicken stock to the boil in a large heavy pan. Add the chicken breasts and bring back to the boil. Reduce the heat and cook for 12–15 minutes, until the chicken breasts are cooked through and tender. Use a draining spoon to remove the chicken from the pan and leave to cool. Reserve the stock.

2 Melt the butter in a pan. Add the onions and cook for 4–5 minutes, until they are softened but not browned.

3 Add the bacon and cook for 5–6 minutes, until it is starting to brown. Add the flour and cook for 1 minute, stirring. Gradually stir in the hot stock and bring to the boil, stirring until the mixture is thickened. Remove from the heat.

4 Stir in the corn and half the milk. Return the pan to the heat and cook, stirring occasionally, for 12–15 minutes until the corn is tender.

5 Cut the chicken into bitesize pieces and stir into the soup. Stir in the butter beans and the remaining milk. Bring to the boil and cook for 5 minutes, season well with salt and freshly ground black pepper and stir in the chopped parsley.

NUTRITIONAL INFORMATION: Energy 570kcal/2395kJ; Protein 52.6g; Carbohydrate 44.6g, of which sugars 16.6g; Fat 21.4g, of which saturates 10.3g; Cholesterol 155mg; Calcium 159mg; Fibre 7.3g; Sodium 1119mg.

Chicken and Lentil Broth

An old-fashioned soup, this version is given more body by adding Puy lentils.

ingredients

SERVES FOUR

- 2 leeks, cut into 5cm/2in fine julienne strips
- 115g/4oz/½ cup Puy lentils
- 2 bay leaves
- few sprigs of fresh thyme
- 2 skinless, boneless chicken breasts
- 900ml/1½ pints/3¾ cups good chicken stock
- 8 ready-to-eat prunes, cut into strips
- salt and ground black pepper
- fresh thyme sprigs, to garnish

1 Boil a small pan of salted water and cook the julienne of leeks for 1–2 minutes. Drain and refresh under cold running water. Drain again and set aside.

cook's tip

Julienne is a name for foods, usually vegetables, cut into long, thin strips. For perfect julienne leeks, cut them into 5cm/2in lengths. Cut each piece in half lengthways, then with the cut side down, slice the leek into thin strips.

2 Put the lentils into a pan with the bay leaves, thyme and water. Bring to the boil and cook for 25 minutes. Drain.

3 Put the chicken breasts in a pan and pour over enough stock to cover them. Bring to the boil

and poach gently for 15–20 minutes until tender. Using a draining spoon, remove the chicken from the stock and leave to cool.

4 When the chicken is cool, cut it into strips. Return it to the pan then add the lentils and remaining stock. Bring to the boil and season.

5 Divide the leeks and prunes among four bowls. Ladle over the hot chicken and lentil broth. Garnish with fresh thyme sprigs and serve.

NUTRITIONAL INFORMATION: Energy 210kcal/891kJ; Protein 26.3g; Carbohydrate 23.8g, of which sugars 9.8g; Fat 1.7g, of which saturates 0.3g; Cholesterol 53mg; Calcium 43mg; Fibre 5g; Sodium 52mg.

Thai Chicken Soup

This Thai-inspired soup is complemented by a topping of crisp shallots and basil leaves.

ingredients

SERVES SIX

- 40g/1½oz/3 tbsp butter
- 1 onion, finely chopped
- 2 garlic cloves, chopped
- 2.5cm/1in piece fresh root ginger, finely chopped
- 10ml/2 tsp green curry paste
- 2.5ml/½ tsp turmeric
- 400ml/14fl oz can coconut milk
- 475ml/16fl oz/2 cups chicken stock
- 2 lime leaves, shredded
- 1 lemon grass stalk, finely chopped
- 8 skinless, boneless chicken thighs
- 350g/12oz spinach, chopped
- 10ml/2 tsp fish sauce
- 30ml/2 tbsp lime juice
- 30ml/2 tbsp vegetable oil
- 2 shallots, thinly sliced
- salt and ground black pepper
- handful of Thai basil leaves, to garnish

1 Melt the butter in a heavy pan. Add the onion, garlic and ginger, then cook for 4–5 minutes. Stir in the curry paste and turmeric, and cook for a further 2–3 minutes, stirring.

2 Pour in two-thirds of the coconut milk and cook for 5 minutes. Add the stock, lime leaves, lemon grass and chicken. Simmer for 15 minutes or until the chicken is tender.

3 Remove the chicken thighs with a draining spoon and set them aside to cool.

4 Add the spinach to the pan and cook for 3–4 minutes. Stir in the remaining coconut milk, then process the soup in a food processor or blender until it is almost smooth. Return the soup to the rinsed-out pan.

5 Cut the chicken thighs into bitesize pieces and stir these into the soup with the fish sauce, lime juice and seasoning.

6 Reheat the soup gently until hot, but do not let it boil. Meanwhile, heat the oil in a frying pan and cook the shallots for 6–8 minutes, until crisp and golden, stirring occasionally. Drain on kitchen paper. Ladle the soup into bowls, then top with the basil leaves and fried shallots, and serve.

NUTRITIONAL INFORMATION: Energy 198kcal/827kJ; Protein 16.5g; Carbohydrate 6.5g, of which sugars 5.5g; Fat 12g, of which saturates 4.6g; Cholesterol 84mg; Calcium 157mg; Fibre 2.3g; Sodium 266mg.

Chicken and Chilli Soup

Ginger and lemon grass add a distinctive Thai flavour to this tasty, refreshing dish.

ingredients

SERVES FOUR

- 150g/5oz skinless, boneless chicken breasts, cut into strips
- 2.5cm/1in piece fresh root ginger, finely chopped
- 5cm/2in piece lemon grass stalk, finely chopped
- 1 fresh red chilli, seeded and thinly sliced
- 8 baby corn cobs, halved lengthways
- 1 large carrot, cut into thin sticks
- 1 litre/1¾ pints/4 cups hot chicken stock
- 4 spring onions (scallions), thinly sliced
- 12 small shiitake mushrooms, sliced
- 115g/4oz/1 cup vermicelli rice noodles
- 30ml/2 tbsp soy sauce
- salt and ground black pepper

1 Place the chicken strips, chopped fresh root ginger, finely chopped lemon grass and sliced chilli in a casserole. Add the halved baby corn and the carrot sticks. Pour over the hot chicken stock and cover the casserole.

2 Place in a cold oven. Set the temperature to 200°C/400°F/ Gas 6 and cook for 30–40 minutes, until the chicken and vegetables are tender.

3 Add the spring onions and mushrooms, cover and return the casserole to the oven for 10 minutes. Place the noodles in a bowl and cover with boiling water. Soak for the time stated on the packet.

4 Drain the noodles and divide among four warmed serving bowls. Stir the soy sauce into the soup and season to taste with salt and pepper. Divide the soup among the bowls and serve.

cook's tip

The soft vermicelli rice noodles are the perfect foil to the vegetables.

NUTRITIONAL INFORMATION: Energy 165kcal/693kJ; Protein 13.3g; Carbohydrate 26g, of which sugars 3.1g; Fat 0.9g, of which saturates 0.2g; Cholesterol 26mg; Calcium 23mg; Fibre 1.4g; Sodium 852mg.

Bacon Broth

A hearty meal in a soup bowl. The bacon hock contributes fantastic flavour and depth to this soup.

ingredients

SERVES SIX TO EIGHT

- 1 bacon hock, about 900g/2lb
- 75g/3oz/½ cup pearl barley
- 75g/3oz/½ cup lentils
- 2 leeks, sliced, or onions, diced
- 4 carrots, diced
- 200g/7oz swede (rutabaga), diced
- 3 potatoes, diced
- small bunch of herbs (e.g. thyme, parsley, bay leaf)
- 1 small cabbage, trimmed and quartered or sliced
- salt and ground black pepper
- chopped fresh parsley, to garnish
- brown bread, to serve

1 Soak the bacon hock in cold water overnight. Drain and put it into a large pan with enough water to cover. Bring to the boil, skim off any scum, and then add the barley and the lentils. Bring back to the boil and simmer for 15 minutes.

2 Add the leeks or onions, carrots, swede, potatoes and herbs to the pan. Bring the broth back to the boil, then reduce the heat and cover the pan, leaving a small space for steam to escape. Simmer for 1½ hours, until the meat is tender.

3 Using a slotted spoon, lift the bacon hock from the pan. Remove the skin, then take the meat off the bones and cut it into bitesize pieces. Return the meat to the pan then add the cabbage. Discard the

mixed herbs. Bring back to the boil, reduce the heat then simmer until the cabbage is cooked to your liking.

4 Season and ladle into large serving bowls. Garnish with chopped parsley and serve with warmed brown bread.

cook's tip

Traditionally, the cabbage is quartered, although it may be sliced if you prefer.

NUTRITIONAL INFORMATION: Energy 306kcal/1284kJ; Protein 17.7g; Carbohydrate 33.5g, of which sugars 8.3g; Fat 12.1g, of which saturates 4.3g; Cholesterol 35mg; Calcium 74mg; Fibre 4.6g; Sodium 1050g.

Pea, Bacon and Barley Soup

This thick soup makes a substantial appetizer or may be served as a meal on its own.

ingredients

SERVES SIX

- 225g/8oz/1¼ cups yellow split peas, rinsed in cold water
- 25g/1oz/¼ cup pearl barley, rinsed in cold water
- 1.75 litres/3 pints/7½ cups vegetable or ham stock
- 50g/2oz smoked streaky (fatty) bacon, cubed
- 25g/1oz/2 tbsp butter
- 1 onion, finely chopped
- 2 garlic cloves, crushed
- 225g/8oz celeriac, cubed
- 15ml/1 tbsp roughly chopped fresh marjoram
- salt and ground black pepper
- bread, to serve

1 Put the peas and barley in a bowl, cover with plenty of water and soak overnight.

2 Drain and rinse the peas and barley. Put them in a pan, add the stock and bring to the boil. Simmer 40 minutes.

3 Dry fry the bacon cubes in a large heavy frying pan for 5 minutes, or until they are well browned and crispy. Remove from the pan with a slotted spoon, leaving the fat behind, and set aside.

4 Add the butter to the frying pan. When it is melted, add the onion and garlic and cook gently for 5 minutes. Add the celeriac and cook for a further 5 minutes, or until the onion is just starting to colour. Do not allow the onion to turn brown as it will affect the taste.

5 Add the softened vegetables and bacon to the pan of stock, peas and barley. Season lightly with salt and ground black pepper, then cover and simmer for 20 minutes, or until the soup is thick. Stir in the marjoram, add extra black pepper to taste and serve with fresh crusty bread.

cook's tip

The bacon is salty, so taste before seasoning, and add salt only if required.

NUTRITIONAL INFORMATION: Energy 189kcal/799kJ; Protein 11g; Carbohydrate 25.8g, of which sugars 1.8g; Fat 5.5g, of which saturates 2.8g; Cholesterol 13mg; Calcium 39mg; Fibre 2.4g; Sodium 190mg.

Gammon and Potato Broth

In this hearty soup, the potatoes cook in the gammon stock, absorbing its flavour and saltiness.

ingredients

SERVES FOUR

- 450g/1lb gammon (smoked or cured ham), in one piece
- 2 bay leaves
- 2 onions, sliced
- 10ml/2 tsp paprika
- 675g/1½lb baking potatoes, cut into large chunks
- 225g/8oz spring greens (collards)
- 425g/15oz can haricot (navy) or cannellini beans, drained
- salt and ground black pepper

1 Soak the gammon overnight in cold water. Drain and put in a large pan with the bay leaves and onions. Pour in 1.5 litres/2½ pints/6¼ cups cold water. Bring to the boil, reduce the heat and simmer very gently for about 1½ hours until the meat is tender.

2 Remove the meat from the pan and cool slightly. Discard skin and excess fat and cut the meat into small chunks. Return to the pan with the paprika and potatoes. Bring back to the boil, reduce the heat, cover and simmer for 20 minutes until the potatoes are tender.

3 Trim the greens. Roll up the leaves and cut into thin shreds with a sharp knife. Add the shredded greens to the pan with the beans. Bring to the boil then reduce the heat and simmer, uncovered, for about 10 minutes. Remove the bay leaves. Season with salt and pepper and serve hot.

variation

Bacon knuckle can be used instead of the gammon (smoked or cured ham) – it is economical and the bones will give the stock a delicious flavour. Freeze any stock you don't use.

cook's tip

Peel the potatoes if you prefer, but the flavour is best with the skin left on. Take care not to add too much salt and spoil the soup. Green cabbage can be substituted for the spring greens, if unavailable.

NUTRITIONAL INFORMATION: Energy 405kcal/1703kJ; Protein 31.7g Carbohydrate 48.8g, of which sugars 8.2g; Fat 10.5g, of which saturates 3.2g; Cholesterol 26mg; Calcium 216mg; Fibre 10g; Sodium 1411mg.

Smoked Gammon Soup

This classic Spanish soup features haricot beans with young turnips.

SERVES SIX

- 150g/5oz/⅔ cup haricot (navy) beans, soaked overnight in water
- 1kg/2¼lb smoked gammon (smoked or cured ham) hock
- 3 potatoes, quartered
- 3 small turnips, sliced in rounds
- 150g/5oz purple sprouting broccoli
- salt and ground black pepper

rind, fat and gristle. Dice half the gammon. Reserve the rest for another recipe.

4 Add the meat to the pan. Discard the stalks from the broccoli and add the leaves and florets to the broth.

5 Simmer the soup for about 10 minutes. Season with ground black pepper, then remove the bone and leave the soup to stand for at least half a day. Reheat well before serving.

1 Put the drained beans and gammon into a large, heavy pan and cover with 2 litres/3½ pints/8 cups water. Slowly bring to the boil, skim off any scum, then turn down the heat and cook gently, covered, for 1¼ hours.

2 Drain, reserving the broth. Return the broth to the pan and add the potatoes, turnips and drained beans.

3 Meanwhile, strip all the gammon off the bone and return the bone to the broth. Discard the

cook's tip

The leftover gammon can be used in pilaffs, risottos and vegetable dishes, or it can be added to Spanish omelettes (tortillas).

NUTRITIONAL INFORMATION: Energy 242kcal/1020kJ; Protein 22.6g; Carbohydrate 23.4g, of which sugars 3g; Fat 7.1g, of which saturates 2.3g; Cholesterol 19mg; Calcium 61mg; Fibre 5.8g; Sodium 751mg.

Rice Porridge with Salt Pork

Originally from China, this dish has now spread throughout Asia and is a favourite comfort food.

ingredients

SERVES TWO

- 900ml/1½ pints/3¾ cups vegetable stock
- 200g/7oz/1¾ cups cooked rice
- 225g/8oz minced (ground) pork
- 15ml/1 tbsp fish sauce
- 2 heads pickled garlic, finely chopped
- 1 celery stick, finely diced
- salt and ground black pepper

To garnish

- 30ml/2 tbsp groundnut (peanut) oil
- 4 garlic cloves, thinly sliced
- 4 small red shallots, sliced

1 Make the garnishes by heating the groundnut oil in a heavy frying pan or non-stick wok and cooking the garlic and shallots over a low heat until brown. Drain well on kitchen paper and reserve for the soup.

2 Pour the stock into a large pan. Bring to the boil and add the rice. Add the minced pork. by taking small teaspoons and tapping the spoon on the side of the pan so that the meat falls into the soup in small lumps.

3 Stir in the fish sauce and pickled garlic and simmer for about 10 minutes, until the pork is cooked. Stir in the diced celery and season to taste.

4 Spoon the rice porridge into two individual warmed bowls. Sprinkle the prepared garlic and

shallots on top of each then season to taste with plenty of ground black pepper. Serve the soup immediately.

cook's tip

- *This dish is often served with flavourful accompaniments such as garlic and shallots.*

- *Pickled garlic has a distinctive flavour and is available in Asian food stores. Once opened, it keeps for a month in the refrigerator.*

NUTRITIONAL INFORMATION: Energy 152kcal/636kJ; Protein 15.2g; Carbohydrate 17g, of which sugars 1.8g; Fat 2.5g, of which saturates 0.3g; Cholesterol 34mg; Calcium 12mg; Fibre 0.3g; Sodium 45mg.

Kale, Chorizo and Potato Soup

This substantial winter soup derives a spicy kick from the chorizo sausage.

ingredients

SERVES SIX TO EIGHT
- 225g/8oz kale, stems removed
- 225g/8oz chorizo sausages
- 675g/1½lb potatoes, cut into chunks
- 1.75 litres/3 pints/7½ cups vegetable stock
- 5ml/1 tsp ground black pepper
- pinch of cayenne pepper (optional)
- 12 slices French bread, toasted on both sides
- salt and ground black pepper

1 Place the kale in a food processor or blender and process to chop it finely or shred it by hand.

2 Prick the sausages and place them in a pan with enough water to cover. Bring just to boiling point, then reduce the heat immediately before the water boils too rapidly and simmer for about 15 minutes. Drain and cut the sausages into thin slices.

3 Boil the potatoes for about 15 minutes or until the chunks are just tender. Drain, and place in a bowl, then mash with a little of the cooking liquid to form a thick paste.

4 Bring the vegetable stock to the boil and add the kale. Bring back to the boil. Reduce the heat and add the chorizo, then simmer gently for about 5 minutes. Gradually add the potato paste, stirring it into the soup, and simmer for 20 minutes. Add the black pepper and cayenne, and salt to taste.

5 Divide the freshly made toast among six to eight serving bowls. Pour the soup over and serve immediately.

cook's tip

The soup gains in flavour if it is made the day before, cooled and chilled overnight, then reheated well before serving.

NUTRITIONAL INFORMATION: Energy 411kcal/1740kJ; Protein 13.2g; Carbohydrate 69.3g, of which sugars 6.2g; Fat 11g, of which saturates 4.1g; Cholesterol 15mg; Calcium 140mg; Fibre 4g; Sodium 812mg.

Sausage and Pesto Soup

This is a satisfying soup with overtones of summer, thanks to the pesto and fresh basil.

ingredients

SERVES FOUR

- 15ml/1 tbsp olive oil, plus extra for frying
- 1 red onion chopped
- 450g/1lb smoked pork sausages
- 225g/3oz/1 cup red lentils
- 400g/14oz can chopped tomatoes
- 1 litre/1¾ pints/4 cups water
- vegetable oil, for deep-frying
- salt and ground black pepper
- 60ml/4 tbsp pesto and fresh basil sprigs to garnish

1 Heat the olive oil in a large, heavy pan and cook the onion until soft but not browned. Coarsely chop all the sausages except for two, and add them to the pan. Cook for 5 minutes.

2 Stir in the lentils, tomatoes and water, and bring to the boil. Reduce the heat, cover and simmer for about 20 minutes. Allow to cool slightly.

3 Purée the sausage mixture in a food processor or blender until smooth. Return to the rinsed-out pan.

4 Cook the remaining sausages in a little oil in a small frying pan for 10 minutes, turning often, until lightly browned and firm. Leave to cool slightly, then slice thinly.

5 Heat the oil for deep-frying to 190°C/375°F or until a cube of day-old bread browns in 60 seconds. Deep-fry the sausages and basil until the sausages are brown and the basil is crisp.

6 Lift the sausages and basil out of the oil and pat dry of fat on kitchen paper.

7 Reheat the soup, add seasoning to taste, then ladle into warmed bowls. Swirl a little pesto through each portion. Sprinkle with the deep-fried sausage slices and basil and serve with warm crusty bread.

cook's tip

Make your own pesto by pounding 90g/3½ oz/1 cup basil leaves, 45ml/3 tbsp Parmesan cheese, 60ml/4 tbsp pine nuts and 120ml/4fl oz/½ cup olive oil together.

NUTRITIONAL INFORMATION: Energy 656kcal/2741kJ; Protein 30.9g; Carbohydrate 46.7g, of which sugars 8.2g; Fat 39.7g, of which saturates 13.1g; Cholesterol 75mg; Calcium 250mg; Fibre 4.8g; Sodium 1109mg.

Country-style Lamb Soup

Traditionally, Irish soda bread is served with this one-pot meal based on classic Irish stew.

ingredients

SERVES FOUR

- 15ml/1 tbsp vegetable oil
- 675g/1½lb boneless lamb chump chops, trimmed and cut into small cubes
- 2 small onions, quartered
- 2 leeks, thickly sliced
- 1 litre/1¾ pints/4 cups lamb stock or water
- 2 large potatoes, cut into chunks
- 2 carrots, thickly sliced
- sprig of fresh thyme, plus extra to garnish
- 15g/½oz/1 tbsp butter
- 30ml/2 tbsp chopped fresh parsley
- salt and ground black pepper
- Irish soda bread, to serve

1 Heat the oil in a pan. Add the lamb and brown in batches. Use a slotted spoon to remove the lamb from the pan.

2 Add the onions and cook for 4–5 minutes, until browned. Return the meat to the pan and add the leeks. Pour in the stock or water, then bring to the boil. Reduce the heat, cover and simmer gently for about 1 hour.

3 Add the potatoes, carrots and thyme, and continue cooking for a further 40 minutes, until the lamb is tender. Remove from the heat and leave to stand for 5 minutes to allow the fat to cool and to settle on the surface of the soup.

4 Skim off the fat. Pour off the stock from the soup into a clean pan and whisk in the butter. Stir in the parsley and season well with salt and freshly ground black pepper, and then pour the liquid back over the soup ingredients.

5 Ladle the soup into warmed bowls and garnish with sprigs of fresh thyme. Serve with Irish soda bread.

variation

The vegetables in this rustic soup can be varied according to the season. Swede (rutabaga), turnip, celeriac or cabbage could be added in place of some of the listed vegetables. If soda bread is not available, try Granary or wholemeal (whole-wheat).

NUTRITIONAL INFORMATION: Energy 500kcal/2092kJ; Protein 38.2g; Carbohydrate 30.2g, of which sugars 12.2g; Fat 26g, of which saturates 11.3g; Cholesterol 136mg; Calcium 104mg; Fibre 6.1g; Sodium 197mg.

Beef and Barley Soup

This traditional Irish farmhouse soup makes a wonderfully restorative dish on a cold day.

ingredients

SERVES SIX TO EIGHT

- 450g/1lb stewing beef, such as leg, on the bone
- 2 large onions
- 50g/2oz/¼ cup pearl barley
- 50g/2oz/¼ cup green split peas
- 3 large carrots, chopped
- 2 white turnips, chopped
- 3 celery stalks, chopped
- 1 large or 2 medium leeks, thinly sliced
- salt and ground black pepper
- chopped fresh parsley, to garnish

cook's tips

• *Buying stewing beef on the bone is not easy. Ask the butcher for bones separate from the meat, if necessary. Alternatively, use minced (ground) beef to make a full-flavoured stock or buy ready-made stock.*
• *Adding salt before the split peas are tender will prevent them from softening properly.*
• *The flavour develops if it is made in advance.*

1 Bone the meat and put the bones and half an onion, roughly sliced, into a large pan. Cover with cold water and bring to the boil. Skim, reduce the heat and cover the pan. Simmer for 1½ hours or longer, until required. Do not salt the stock.

2 Trim any fat or gristle from the meat and cut it into small pieces. Chop the remaining onions finely.

3 Strain the stock, discard the bones, and add water to make up to 2 litres/3½ pints/9 cups.

Return the stock to the rinsed-out pan. Add the meat, onions, barley and split peas. Do not add salt yet. Bring to the boil, and skim if necessary. Reduce the heat, cover and simmer for about 30 minutes.

4 Add the rest of the vegetables and simmer for 1 hour, or until the meat is tender. Add seasoning to taste and simmer the soup for a further 5 minutes. Serve in large warmed bowls, generously sprinkled with chopped fresh parsley.

NUTRITIONAL INFORMATION: Energy 194kcal/816kJ; Protein 20.3g; Carbohydrate 21.6g, of which sugars 12g; Fat 3.5g, of which saturates 1.2g; Cholesterol 30mg; Calcium 84mg; Fibre 5g; Sodium 88mg.

Beef Chilli Soup with Nachos

Steaming bowls of beef chilli soup, packed with beans, are delicious topped with crushed tortillas.

ingredients

SERVES FOUR

- 45ml/3 tbsp olive oil
- 350g/12oz rump (round) steak, diced
- 2 onions, chopped
- 2 garlic cloves, crushed
- 2 green chillies seeded and chopped
- 30ml/2 tbsp mild chilli powder
- 5ml/1 tsp ground cumin
- 2 bay leaves
- 30ml/2 tbsp tomato purée (paste)
- 900ml/1½ pints/3¾ cups beef stock
- 2 x 400g/14oz cans mixed beans, drained and rinsed
- 45ml/3 tbsp chopped fresh coriander (cilantro)
- salt and ground black pepper

For the topping

- bag of plain tortilla chips, lightly crushed
- 225g/8oz Monterey Jack or Cheddar cheese, grated

1 Heat the oil in a pan over a high heat and brown the meat. Remove from the pan. Reduce the heat and add the onions, garlic and chillies, then cook for 4–5 minutes, until softened.

2 Stir in the chilli powder and cumin and cook for a further 2 minutes. Return the meat to the pan, then stir in the bay leaves, tomato purée and beef stock. Bring to the boil. Reduce the heat, cover and simmer for about 45 minutes or until the meat is tender and well cooked.

3 Put a quarter of the beans into a bowl and mash well using a potato masher. Stir the mashed beans into the soup to thicken it slightly. Add the remaining beans and simmer for 5 minutes. Taste the soup and add salt and ground black pepper to adjust the seasoning.

4 When the soup is ready to serve, stir in the chopped coriander, ladle into bowls and sprinkle the tortilla chips over the surface. Pile the grated cheese over the tortilla chips and serve.

variation

The soup can be finished by putting the bowls under the grill (broiler) to brown the cheese. Make sure you use flameproof bowls.

NUTRITIONAL INFORMATION: Energy 631kcal/2629kJ; Protein 38.7g; Carbohydrate 25.6g, of which sugars 2.5g; Fat 41g, of which saturates 17.7g; Cholesterol 103mg; Calcium 500mg; Fibre 4.5g; Sodium 788mg.

Oxtail and Leek Soup

This is a Spanish-style oxtail dish – more substantial than broth but with lots of liquid.

ingredients

SERVES SIX

- 30ml/2 tbsp plain (all-purpose) flour
- 1.6kg/3½ lb oxtail, chopped into chunks
- 60ml/4 tbsp olive oil
- 2 onions, chopped
- 6 carrots, cut into short lengths
- 2 large garlic cloves, crushed
- 1 bay leaf
- 2 thyme sprigs
- 2 leeks, sliced thinly
- 1 clove
- pinch of freshly grated nutmeg
- 350ml/12fl oz/1½ cups red wine
- 30ml/2 tbsp vinegar
- 750ml/1¼ pints/3 cups stock
- 30ml/2 tbsp fino sherry
- boiled potatoes (optional)
- 60ml/4 tbsp chopped fresh parsley
- salt, paprika and black pepper

1 Season the flour with salt, paprika and pepper, and dust the oxtail pieces all over. Heat the oil. Brown the oxtail pieces in batches. Remove them as they are ready.

2 Add the onions, carrots, garlic, bay leaf, thyme sprigs and leeks. Cook, stirring, for about 5 minutes. Stir in the clove, grated nutmeg and more black pepper.

3 Put the oxtail back in the pan, nesting the pieces among the vegetables. Pour in the wine, vinegar and enough stock to cover the meat and vegetables. Bring to simmering point, then cover and simmer very gently, stirring occasionally, for 3 hours, or longer, until the meat is falling off the bones.

4 Lift out the oxtail and cut all the meat off the bones. Skim the fat off the stock. Discard the bay leaf and thyme. Spoon the garlic and some of the soft vegetables into a food processor or blender and purée with the sherry.

5 Return the meat and purée to the pan. Add the boiled potatoes, if using, and heat through. Stir in the chopped fresh parsley, check the seasoning and ladle into bowls to serve.

NUTRITIONAL INFORMATION: Energy 416kcal/1737kJ; Protein 33.4g; Carbohydrate 12.2g, of which sugars 6.1g; Fat 21.5g, of which saturates 1.1g; Cholesterol 159mg; Calcium 63mg; Fibre 2.6g; Sodium 201mg.

Meatballs and Pasta Soup

This hearty soup is a meal in itself, with meatballs, beans, pasta and fresh vegetables.

ingredients

SERVES FOUR

- 400g/14oz can cannellini beans, drained and rinsed
- 1 litre/1¾ pints/4 cups vegetable stock
- 45ml/3 tbsp olive oil
- 1 onion, finely chopped
- 2 garlic cloves, chopped
- 1 small fresh red chilli, seeded and finely chopped
- 2 celery sticks, finely chopped
- 1 carrot, finely chopped
- 15ml/1 tbsp tomato purée (paste)
- 300g/11oz pasta shapes
- large handful of fresh basil
- salt and ground black pepper
- basil leaves, to garnish
- freshly grated Parmesan cheese, to serve

For the meatballs

- 1 slice white bread, crusts removed, made into crumbs
- 60ml/4 tbsp milk
- 350g/12oz lean minced (ground) beef
- 30ml/2 tbsp chopped fresh parsley
- grated rind of 1 orange
- 2 garlic cloves, crushed
- 1 egg, beaten
- 30ml/2 tbsp olive oil

1 For the meatballs, mix the bread, milk, meat, parsley, orange rind, garlic, egg and seasoning. Stand for 15 minutes, then shape into balls about the size of a large olive.

2 Heat the oil in a frying pan and fry in batches, all over, for 6–8 minutes each. Remove from the pan and set aside.

3 Purée the cannellini beans with a little of the vegetable stock in a food processor or blender until the mixture is smooth. Set aside.

4 Heat the olive oil in a pan. Add the onion, garlic, chilli, celery and carrot. Cover and cook gently for 10 minutes, then stir in the tomato purée, bean purée and the remaining stock. Bring the soup to the boil and cook for about 10 minutes.

5 Stir in the pasta and simmer for 8–10 minutes, until the pasta is tender. Add the meatballs and basil and cook for 5 minutes. Season and ladle into warmed bowls. Garnish with basil and serve with grated Parmesan cheese.

NUTRITIONAL INFORMATION: Energy 277kcal/1158kJ; Protein 19.9g; Carbohydrate 20.5g, of which sugars 1.4g; Fat 14g, of which saturates 6.1g; Cholesterol 89mg; Calcium 133mg; Fibre 1g; Sodium 731mg.

Beef Dumpling Soup

Succulent dumplings taste fantastic in this simple but delicious broth.

cook's tips

- The quality of stock and dumplings is important for the success of this soup, so start with good home-made stock or superior bought stock. Be guided by price when buying dumplings and check the label for filling ingredients: cheap dumplings usually have inferior filling.
- If you want to use fresh dumplings, cook them for 5 minutes.
- Soy sauce with a drop of vinegar makes a good dipping sauce for the dumplings.
- When cooking dumplings don't stir the soup or stir it very carefully, to avoid causing the dumplings to tear and release the filling.

1 Place the beef stock in a pan and bring to the boil. Add the frozen dumplings, cover, and boil for 6 minutes.

2 Using a sharp knife, finely slice the spring onion and chilli. Crush the garlic clove then add the spring onion, chilli and garlic to the pan with the soy sauce. Simmer for a further 2 minutes.

3 Season with salt and pepper to taste, and serve piping hot.

variation

Use chicken stock and prawn (shrimp) or pork-filled dumplings. Add a little finely shredded crisp lettuce and grated lemon rind to each bowl when serving.

NUTRITIONAL INFORMATION: Energy 106kcal/445kJ; Protein 2g; Carbohydrate 12.6g of which sugars 0.6g; Fat 6.1g, of which saturates 3.4g; Cholesterol 5mg; Calcium 30mg; Fibre 0.5g; Sodium 842mg.

Mackerel and Tomato Soup

All the ingredients for this unusual soup are cooked in a single pan, so it is quick and easy to prepare.

ingredients

SERVES FOUR

- 200g/7oz smoked mackerel fillets
- 4 tomatoes
- 1 litre/1¾ pints/4 cups vegetable stock
- 1 lemon grass stalk, chopped
- 5cm/2in piece fresh galangal or root ginger, finely diced or sliced
- 4 shallots, finely chopped
- 2 garlic cloves, finely chopped
- 2.5ml/½ tsp dried chilli flakes
- 15ml/1 tbsp fish sauce
- 5ml/1 tsp palm sugar (jaggery) or light muscovado (brown) sugar
- 45ml/3 tbsp thick tamarind juice, made by mixing tamarind paste with warm water
- small bunch fresh chives or spring onions (scallions), to garnish

1 Prepare the smoked mackerel fillets. Remove and discard the skin, then chop the flesh into large pieces. Carefully remove any stray bones.

2 Cut the tomatoes in half, squeeze out and discard most of the seeds, then finely dice the flesh with a sharp knife. Place in a bowl and set aside.

3 Pour the stock into a large pan and add the lemon grass, galangal or ginger, shallots and garlic. Bring to the boil then simmer for 15 minutes.

4 Add the fish, tomatoes, chilli flakes, fish sauce, sugar and tamarind juice. Bring back to simmering point, then continue to simmer for around 4–5 minutes, until the fish and tomatoes are heated through.

5 Ladle the soup into bowls, garnish with chives or spring onions and serve.

cook's tip

Smoked mackerel adds a robust flavour, tempered by lemon grass and tamarind.

NUTRITIONAL INFORMATION: Energy 226kcal/940kJ; Protein 11.2g; Carbohydrate 10.2g, of which sugars 8.5g; Fat 15.9g, of which saturates 3.3g; Cholesterol 53mg; Calcium 39mg; Fibre 2.1g; Sodium 653mg.

Cod, Bean and Spinach Chowder

Granary croûtons make a crunchy accompaniment to this delicious and filling chowder.

ingredients

SERVES SIX

- 1 litre/1¾ pints/4 cups milk
- 150ml/¼ pint/⅔ cup double (heavy) cream
- 675g/1½lb cod fillet, skinned and boned
- 45ml/3 tbsp olive oil
- 1 onion, sliced
- 2 garlic cloves, finely chopped
- 450g/1lb potatoes, thickly sliced
- 450g/1lb fresh broad (fava) beans, podded
- 30ml/2 tbsp chopped fresh chives, plus extra to garnish
- 225g/8oz baby spinach leaves
- pinch of grated nutmeg
- salt and ground black pepper
- fresh chives,

For the Granary croûtons

- 30ml/4 tbsp olive oil
- 6 slices Granary (whole-wheat) bread, crusts removed and cut into large cubes

1 Pour the milk and cream into a large, heavy pan and bring to the boil. Add the cod fillet and bring back to the boil. Reduce the heat and simmer for 2–3 minutes, then remove from the heat, cover and leave to stand for about 6 minutes, until the fish is just cooked. Using a slotted spoon, remove the fish from the cooking liquid and place on a chopping board.

2 Using a fork, flake the cooked cod into chunky pieces, remove any bones or skin, then cover and set aside.

3 Heat the olive oil in a large pan and add the onion and garlic. Cook for about 5 minutes until softened. Add the potatoes, stir in the milk mixture and bring to the boil. Reduce the heat and cover. Cook for 10 minutes. Add the broad beans; cook for 10 minutes, until tender.

4 Meanwhile, make the croûtons. Heat the oil in a frying pan and add the bread cubes. Cook over a medium heat, stirring often, until golden all over. Remove and pat dry.

5 Add the cod and chives to the soup and heat through gently. Add the spinach and stir for 1–2 minutes, until wilted. Season and add the nutmeg.

6 Ladle the soup into bowls and pile the croûtons on top. Garnish with chives.

NUTRITIONAL INFORMATION: Energy 603kcal/2525kJ; Protein 37.9g; Carbohydrate 44.7g, of which sugars 12.2g; Fat 31.6g, of which saturates 12.5g; Cholesterol 96mg; Calcium 398mg; Fibre 7.5g; Sodium 375mg.

Curried Salmon Soup

A hint of mild curry paste really enhances the flavour of this soup, without making it too spicy.

ingredients

SERVES FOUR

- 50g/2oz/¼ cup butter
- 2 onions, roughly chopped
- 10ml/2 tsp mild curry paste
- 150ml/¼ pint/⅔ cup white wine
- 300ml/½ pint/1¼ cups double (heavy) cream
- 50g/2oz/½ cup creamed coconut, grated, or 120ml/4fl oz/½ cup coconut cream
- 2 potatoes, about 350g/12oz, cubed
- 450g/1lb salmon fillet, skinned and cut into bitesize pieces
- 60ml/4 tbsp chopped fresh flat leaf parsley
- salt and ground black pepper

1 Melt the butter in a large, heavy pan, add the onions and cook for about 3–4 minutes until they are beginning to soften but do not allow them to turn brown. Stir in the curry paste and cook for another minute more.

2 Add 475ml/16fl oz/2 cups water, the white wine, the double cream and creamed coconut or coconut cream, with salt and ground black pepper to taste. Bring to the boil and keep stirring until the coconut has completely dissolved.

3 Add the cubed potatoes and bring to the boil. Simmer, covered, for about 15 minutes or until they are almost tender. Do not allow them to overcook so that they turn mushy and break down into the liquid.

4 Add the fish and cook gently without breaking it up, for about 2–3 minutes until it is just cooked and flakes easily. Add the parsley and adjust the seasoning with salt and freshly ground black pepper. Serve the soup immediately.

cook's tip

If you want a more spicy taste, you could substitute medium or hot curry paste for the mild variety.

NUTRITIONAL INFORMATION: Energy 837kcal/3466kJ; Protein 26.3g; Carbohydrate 16.6g, of which sugars 3.6g; Fat 71.8g, of which saturates 41.2g; Cholesterol 186mg; Calcium 74mg; Fibre 0.9g; Sodium 158mg.

Haddock and Potato Soup

Cullen Skink is a classic Scottish dish using one of the country's tastiest fish, smoked haddock.

ingredients

SERVES SIX

- 350g/12oz smoked haddock fillet
- 1 onion, chopped
- bouquet garni
- 900ml/1½ pints/3¾ cups water
- 500g/1¼lb floury potatoes, quartered
- 600ml/1 pint/2½ cups milk
- 40g/1½oz/3 tbsp butter
- salt and ground black pepper
- chopped chives to garnish
- crusty bread, to serve

3 Strain the fish stock and return it to the pan. Then add the potatoes and simmer for about 25 minutes until tender. Remove the potatoes from the pan. Add the milk to the pan and bring the soup to the boil.

4 Mash the potatoes with the butter, then whisk the mash into the soup. Add the flaked fish to the pan and heat through gently. Season with salt and pepper to taste then ladle into six bowls, sprinkle with chives and serve with crusty bread.

1 Put the haddock, onion, bouquet garni and water into a heavy pan and bring to the boil. Skim the scum from the surface, then cover, reduce the heat and poach gently for 10–15 minutes, until the haddock flakes easily.

2 Lift the haddock from the pan with a slotted spoon, cool slightly, then remove the skin and bones. Flake the flesh and put to one side. Return the skin and bones to the pan and continue to simmer for a further 30 minutes.

NUTRITIONAL INFORMATION: Energy 205kcal/864kJ; Protein 16.1g; Carbohydrate 19g, of which sugars 6.4g; Fat 7.8g, of which saturates 4.7g; Cholesterol 47mg; Calcium 142mg; Fibre 1g; Sodium 536mg.

Fish Soup with Rouille

This traditional French soup has a rich flavour and a beautifully smooth texture.

ingredients

SERVES SIX

- 1kg/2¼lb mixed fish, filleted
- 30ml/2 tbsp olive oil
- 1 each onion, carrot and leek, chopped
- 2 large tomatoes, chopped
- 1 red (bell) pepper, seeded and chopped
- 2 garlic cloves, peeled
- 150g/5oz/⅔ cup tomato purée (paste)
- 300ml/½ pint/1¼ cups dry white wine
- salt and ground black pepper

For the rouille
- 2 garlic cloves, chopped
- 5ml/1 tsp coarse salt
- 1 thick slice of white bread, crust removed, soaked in water and squeezed dry
- 1 red chilli, seeded and chopped
- 45ml/3 tbsp olive oil
- salt and cayenne pepper

For the garnish
- 12 slices of baguette, toasted in the oven
- 50g/2oz finely grated Gruyère

1 Cut the fish into 7.5cm/3in chunks. Heat the oil, then add the fish and vegetables. Stir until they begin to colour.

2 Add all the other soup ingredients, then pour in just enough cold water to cover. Season, bring to just below boiling point, then lower the heat to a bare simmer, cover and cook for 1 hour.

3 Meanwhile, make the rouille. Put the garlic and coarse salt in a mortar and crush to a paste with a pestle. Add the soaked bread and chilli and pound until smooth. Whisk in the olive oil, a drop at a time, to make a smooth, shiny sauce that resembles mayonnaise. Season with salt and a pinch of cayenne. Set the rouille aside.

4 Purée the soup in batches in a food processor, then strain through a fine sieve (strainer) placed over a clean pan, pushing the solids through with a ladle.

5 Reheat the soup without letting it boil and ladle into individual bowls. Top each serving with two slices of toasted baguette, a spoonful of rouille and a sprinkling of grated Gruyère.

NUTRITIONAL INFORMATION: Energy 518kcal/2179kJ; Protein 41.5g; Carbohydrate 49g, of which sugars 10.8g; Fat 14.9g, of which saturates 3.6g; Cholesterol 85mg; Calcium 193mg; Fibre 4.3g; Sodium 665mg.

Mullet and Fennel Soup

Olives and tomato toasts, rubbed with garlic, are delicious as an accompaniment for this soup.

ingredients

SERVES FOUR

- 25ml/1½ tbsp olive oil
- 1 onion, chopped
- 3 garlic cloves, chopped
- 2 fennel bulbs, thinly sliced
- 4 tomatoes chopped
- 1 bay leaf
- sprig of fresh thyme
- 1.2 litres/2 pints/5 cups fish stock
- 675g/1½lb red mullet or snapper, scaled and filleted
- salt and ground black pepper

For the toasts
- 8 slices baguette, toasted
- 1 garlic clove
- 30ml/2 tbsp tomato purée (paste)
- 12 black olives, pitted
- fresh fennel fronds, to garnish

For the aioli
- 2 egg yolks
- 1–2 garlic cloves, crushed
- 10ml/2 tsp lemon juice
- 300ml/½ pint/1¼ cups extra virgin olive oil

1 Heat the olive oil in a large pan. Add the onion and garlic and cook for 5 minutes. Add the fennel and cook for 2–3 minutes. Stir in the tomatoes, bay leaf, thyme and stock. Boil, reduce the heat, cover and simmer for 30 minutes.

2 Meanwhile, make the aioli. Whisk the egg yolks, garlic, lemon juice and seasoning together. Whisk in the oil, drops at a time. As the mixture begins to thicken, add the oil in a slow trickle. Transfer to a large bowl and set aside.

3 Cut each mullet fillet into two or three pieces, then add them to the soup and cook gently for 5 minutes. Use a slotted spoon to remove the mullet and set aside.

4 Strain the cooking liquid through a sieve (strainer). Whisk a ladleful of soup into the aioli, then whisk in the remaining soup in one go. Return the soup to a clean pan and cook very gently, whisking continuously, until the mixture is very slightly thickened. Add the mullet pieces to the soup.

5 Rub the baguette slices with garlic, spread with tomato purée and top with olives. Serve the soup topped with the toasts and fennel.

NUTRITIONAL INFORMATION: Energy 492kcal/2079kJ; Protein 41.2g; Carbohydrate 53.6g, of which sugars 10g; Fat 14.1g, of which saturates 1.2g; Cholesterol 60mg; Calcium 256mg; Fibre 6.1g; Sodium 965mg.

White Fish Soup with Orange

This Spanish soup, sopa cachorreña, is good served in January, when Seville oranges are in season.

ingredients

SERVES SIX

- 1kg/2¼lb small hake or whiting, whole but cleaned
- 4 bitter oranges or 4 sweet oranges and 2 lemons
- 30ml/2 tbsp olive oil
- 5 garlic cloves, unpeeled
- 1 large onion, finely chopped
- 1 tomato, peeled, seeded and chopped
- 4 small potatoes, cut into rounds
- 5ml/1 tsp paprika
- salt and ground black pepper
- 15–30ml/1–2 tbsp chopped fresh parsley, to garnish

1 Fillet the fish and cut each fillet into three, reserving all the trimmings. Salt the fillets lightly, cover and chill.

2 Prepare the stock. Put the trimmings in a pan, add 1.2 litres/2 pints/5 cups water and some orange rind. Bring to a simmer, skim, then cover and cook for 30 minutes.

3 Heat the oil in a large pan over a high heat. Smash the garlic cloves with the flat of a knife and fry until they are well-coloured. Discard them and turn down the heat. Fry the onion gently until it is softened. Add the tomato to the onion halfway through.

4 Strain in the hot fish stock (adding the orange rind as well if you wish) and bring the soup back to the boil. Add the potatoes to the pan and cook them for about 5 minutes or until they are just tender.

5 Add the fish pieces to the soup, a few at a time, without letting it go off the boil. Cook for about 15 minutes.

6 Squeeze the juice from the fruit and stir into the soup with the paprika. Season to taste with salt and ground black pepper. Ladle into six bowls and serve garnished with a little chopped parsley.

NUTRITIONAL INFORMATION: Energy 263kcal/1105kJ; Protein 27.1g; Carbohydrate 23.9g, of which sugars 12.2g; Fat 7.2g, of which saturates 1.1g; Cholesterol 30mg; Calcium 81mg; Fibre 3.2g; Sodium 155mg.

Monkfish and Coconut Soup

This light coconut soup is based on Thailand's classic stir-fried noodle dish.

ingredients

SERVES FOUR

- 175g/6oz flat rice noodles
- 30ml/2 tbsp vegetable oil
- 2 garlic cloves, chopped
- 15ml/1 tbsp red curry paste
- 450g/1lb monkfish tail, cut into bitesize pieces
- 300ml/½ pint/1¼ cups coconut cream
- 750ml/1¼ pints/3 cups hot chicken stock
- 45ml/3 tbsp Thai fish sauce
- 15ml/1 tbsp palm sugar (jaggery)
- 60ml/4 tbsp roughly chopped roasted peanuts
- 4 spring onions (scallions), shredded lengthways
- 50g/2oz beansprouts
- large handful of fresh Thai basil leaves
- salt and ground black pepper
- 1 red chilli, seeded and cut into slivers, to garnish

1 Soak the noodles in boiling water for 10 minutes, or according to the packet instructions. Drain.

2 Heat the oil in a large pan over a high heat. Add the chopped garlic and cook for about 2 minutes. Stir in the curry paste and cook for another minute.

3 Add the monkfish and stir-fry over a high heat for 4–5 minutes. Pour in the coconut cream and stock. Stir in the fish sauce and sugar, and bring just to the boil. Add the noodles and cook for 1–2 minutes.

4 Stir in half the peanuts, half the spring onions, half the beansprouts, the basil and seasoning. Ladle into bowls and scatter over the remaining peanuts, the rest of the spring onions and beansprouts, and the red chilli.

cook's tip

Thai fish sauce is made from salted, fermented fish.

NUTRITIONAL INFORMATION: Energy 379kcal/1589kJ; Protein 25.5g; Carbohydrate 41.2g, of which sugars 4.7g; Fat 12g, of which saturates 2g; Cholesterol 18mg; Calcium 49mg; Fibre 0.9g; Sodium 111mg.

Clam and Mushroom Chowder

The sweet taste of clams and the earthiness of wild mushrooms combine to make this a great meal.

ingredients

SERVES FOUR

- 48 clams, scrubbed
- 50g/2oz/4 tbsp unsalted (sweet) butter
- 1 large onion, chopped
- 1 celery stick, sliced
- 1 carrot, sliced
- 225g/8oz assorted wild mushrooms, such as chanterelles, saffron milk-caps, chicken of the woods or St George's mushrooms, sliced
- 225g/8oz floury potatoes, thickly sliced
- 1.2 litres/2 pints/5 cups light chicken or vegetable stock, boiling
- 1 thyme sprig
- 4 parsley stalks
- salt and ground black pepper
- fresh thyme, to garnish

1 Place the clams in a large pan, discarding any that are open and do not shut when tapped. Put 1cm/½ in of water in the pan, cover, bring to the boil and steam over a medium heat for 6–8 minutes until the clams open (discard any clams that do not open).

2 Drain the clams over a bowl and remove the shells, reserving a few clams in their shells for garnish. Chop the shelled clams. Strain the cooking juices into the bowl, add the chopped clams and set aside.

3 Add the butter, onion, celery and carrot to the pan and cook for 10 minutes, until the vegetables are tender.

4 Add the mushrooms and cook for about 3–4 minutes until their juices begin to seep out. Add the potatoes, the clams with their juices, the stock, the thyme sprig and the parsley stalks.

5 Bring the soup to the boil, then reduce the heat, cover and simmer for 25 minutes, stirring occasionally. Season, ladle into bowls and garnish with the reserved clams and fresh thyme.

NUTRITIONAL INFORMATION: Energy 203kcal/848kJ; Protein 10.8g; Carbohydrate 15.8g, of which sugars 5.2g; Fat 11.2g, of which saturates 6.8g; Cholesterol 60mg; Calcium 66mg; Fibre 2.4g; Sodium 696mg.

Saffron-flavoured Mussel Soup

This creamy soup, with the black shells and plump mussels, tastes as delicious as it looks.

ingredients

SERVES FOUR

- 1.5kg/3–3½lb fresh mussels
- 600ml/1 pint /2½ cups white wine
- few fresh parsley stalks
- 50g/2oz/¼ cup butter
- 2 leeks, finely chopped
- 2 celery sticks, finely chopped
- 1 carrot, chopped
- 2 garlic cloves, chopped
- large pinch of saffron threads
- 600ml/1 pint/2½ cups double (heavy) cream
- 3 tomatoes, peeled, seeded and chopped
- 30ml/2 tbsp chopped chives, to garnish

1 Scrub the mussels and pull away the beards. Discard any that are open and do not close when tapped. Put the mussels into a large pan with the wine and parsley stalks. Cover, bring to the boil and cook for 4–5 minutes, shaking the pan occasionally, until the mussels have opened. Discard the parsley stalks and any mussels that are not open.

2 Drain the mussels over a large bowl, reserving the cooking liquid for the soup.

3 When cool enough to handle, remove half of the cooked mussels from their shells. Set aside and reserve the remaining mussels in their shells for garnish.

4 Melt the butter in a large pan and add the leeks, celery, carrot and garlic, and cook for 5 minutes until softened. Strain the reserved mussel cooking liquid through a fine sieve. Add to the pan and cook over a high heat for 8–10 minutes to reduce. Strain into a clean pan, add the saffron threads and cook for 1 minute.

4 Add the cream and bring back to the boil. Season. Add all the mussels and the tomatoes and heat gently. Ladle the soup into bowls, sprinkle with the chives and garnish with the reserved mussels.

NUTRITIONAL INFORMATION: Energy 441kcal/1825kJ; Protein 9.6g; Carbohydrate 3.1g, of which sugars 3.1g; Fat 39.1g, of which saturates 23.9g; Cholesterol 176mg; Calcium 137mg; Fibre 0.6g; Sodium 156mg.

Crab, Coconut and Chilli Soup

This soup has all the flavours associated with the Bahia region of Brazil, from where it originates.

ingredients

SERVES FOUR

- 30ml/2 tbsp olive oil
- 1 onion, finely chopped
- 1 celery stick, finely chopped
- 2 garlic cloves, crushed
- 1 fresh red chilli, seeded and chopped
- 1 large tomato, peeled and chopped
- 45ml/3 tbsp chopped fresh coriander (cilantro)
- 1 litre/1¾ pints/4 cups fresh crab or fish stock
- 500g/1¼lb crab meat
- 250ml/8fl oz/1 cup coconut milk
- 30ml/2 tbsp palm oil
- juice of 1 lime
- salt
- hot chilli oil, to serve
- lime wedges, to serve

1 Heat the olive oil in a large, heavy pan over a low heat. Stir in the chopped onion and celery, and sauté gently for 5 minutes, until softened. Stir in the garlic and chilli and cook for a further 2 minutes.

2 Add the tomato and half the coriander and increase the heat. Cook, stirring, for about 3

minutes, then add the stock. Bring to the boil, then reduce the heat and simmer the mixture for a further 5 minutes.

3 Stir the crab, coconut milk and palm oil into the pan and simmer over a very low heat for

a further 5 minutes. The consistency should be fairly thick, but not as thick as a stew, so add some water to thin the mixture if needed.

4 Stir in the lime juice and the remaining coriander, then season with salt. Serve the soup with the chilli oil and plenty of lime wedges on the side for squeezing.

variation

Try chunks of white fish fillet instead of crab for a change.

NUTRITIONAL INFORMATION: Energy 228kcal/951kJ; Protein 23.6g; Carbohydrate 5.4g, of which sugars 5g; Fat 12.6g, of which saturates 3.7g; Cholesterol 90mg; Calcium 199mg; Fibre 1.1g; Sodium 767mg.

Chinese Crab and Corn Soup

There's no denying the delightful combination of shellfish and corn in this universal favourite.

ingredients

SERVES FOUR

- 600ml/1 pint/2½ cups fish or chicken stock
- 2.5cm/1in piece fresh root ginger, peeled and very finely sliced
- 400g/14oz can creamed corn
- 150g/5oz cooked white crab meat
- 15ml/1 tbsp arrowroot or cornflour (cornstarch)
- 15ml/1 tbsp rice wine or dry sherry
- 15–30ml/1–2 tbsp light soy sauce
- 1 egg white
- salt and ground white pepper
- shredded spring onions (scallions), to garnish

1 Put the stock and ginger in a large pan and bring to the boil. Reduce the heat a little while you stir in the creamed corn, then bring the mixture back to the boil.

2 Remove from the heat and add the crab meat to the pan. Put the arrowroot or cornflour in a cup and stir in the rice wine or sherry to make a smooth paste; stir this into the soup. Cook over a low heat, stirring, for about 3 minutes until the

soup has thickened and is slightly glutinous in consistency. Add light soy sauce, salt and white pepper to taste.

3 In a bowl, whisk the egg white to a stiff foam. Gradually fold it into the soup. Ladle the soup into heated bowls, garnish with spring onions and serve.

cook's tip

This soup is sometimes made with whole kernel corn, but creamed corn gives a better texture. If you can't find it in a can, use thawed frozen creamed corn instead; the result will be just as good.

variation

Instead of crab, use 150g/5oz peeled prawns (shrimp).

NUTRITIONAL INFORMATION: Energy 201kcal/852kJ; Protein 11.3g; Carbohydrate 33.8g, of which sugars 9.9g; Fat 3.2g, of which saturates 0.5g; Cholesterol 27mg; Calcium 17mg; Fibre 1.4g; Sodium 695mg.

Lobster Bisque

Bisque is a luxurious, velvety soup which can be made with any crustacean, such as crab or shrimp.

ingredients

SERVES SIX

- 500g/1¼ lb fresh lobster
- 75g/3oz/6 tbsp butter
- 1 onion, chopped
- 1 carrot, diced
- 1 celery stick, diced
- 45ml/3 tbsp brandy
- 250ml/8fl oz/1 cup dry white wine
- 1 litre/1¾ pints/4 cups fish stock
- 15ml/1 tbsp tomato purée (paste)
- 75g/3oz/scant ½ cup long grain rice
- 1 fresh bouquet garni
- 150ml/¼ pint/⅔ cup double (heavy) cream, plus extra to garnish
- salt, ground white pepper and cayenne pepper

1 Cut the lobster into pieces. Melt half the butter in a large pan, add the vegetables and cook over a low heat until soft. Put in the lobster and stir gently until the shells turn red.

2 Add the brandy and set it alight. When the flames die down, add the wine and boil until reduced by half. Add the fish stock and simmer for 2–3 minutes. Remove the lobster.

3 Add the tomato purée, rice and bouquet garni, and cook until the rice is tender. Remove the meat from the shell and return the shells to the pan. Dice the meat and set it aside.

4 When the rice is cooked, discard the larger bits of shell. Whizz the mixture to a purée in a blender or food processor. Press the purée through a fine sieve (strainer) over the clean pan. Heat until almost boiling. Season with salt, pepper and cayenne.

5 Lower the heat and stir in the cream. Dice the remaining butter and whisk it into the bisque. Add the diced lobster meat and serve at once. If you like, pour a small spoonful of brandy into each soup bowl and swirl in a little extra cream.

cook's tip

If you want to use a cooked lobster, take care not to overcook the flesh. Stir for only 30–60 seconds.

NUTRITIONAL INFORMATION: Energy 347kcal/1438kJ; Protein 8.5g; Carbohycrate 12.9g, of which sugars 2.6g; Fat 24.3g, of which saturates 15g; Cholesterol 94mg; Calcium 48mg; Fibre 0.6g; Sodium 195mg.

Prawn Tail Broth with Wontons

This classic Chinese snack is popular on fast-food stalls throughout the regions of southern China.

ingredients

SERVES FOUR

- 200g/7oz minced (ground) pork
- 200g/7oz peeled cooked prawns (shrimp), thawed if frozen
- 10ml/2 tsp rice wine or dry sherry
- 10ml/2 tsp light soy sauce
- 5ml/1 tsp sesame oil
- 24 thin wonton wrappers
- 1.2 litres/2 pints/5 cups chicken stock
- 12 raw tiger prawns (jumbo shrimp), shelled, with tails
- 350g/12oz pak choi (bok choy), coarsely shredded
- salt and ground black pepper

For the garnish

- 4 spring onions (scallions), sliced
- 1cm/½in piece fresh root ginger, finely shredded

1 Put the pork, prawns, rice wine or sherry, soy sauce and sesame oil in a large bowl. Add plenty of seasoning and mix the ingredients thoroughly.

2 Put about 10ml/2 tsp of the pork mixture in the centre of each wonton wrapper. Bring up the sides of the wrapper and pinch them together to seal the filling in a small bundle.

3 Bring a pan of water to the boil. Add the wontons and simmer for 3 minutes, then drain well and set aside.

4 Pour the stock into a large pan and bring to the boil. Season, add the tiger prawns and cook for 2–3 minutes. Add the wontons and shredded pak choi to the stock, then simmer the soup for a further 1–2 minutes until the green vegetables are wilted and the wontons are completely heated through.

5 Ladle the soup into four bowls. Garnish with spring onions and ginger. Serve.

NUTRITIONAL INFORMATION: Energy 273kcal/1148kJ; Protein 32.1g; Carbohydrate 21g, of which sugars 1.9g; Fat 7.2g, of which saturates 2.2g; Cholesterol 228mg; Calcium 267mg; Fibre 2.6g; Sodium 524mg.

Spicy Prawn and Squash Soup

This highly flavoured soup comes from northern Thailand. It is a cross between a soup and a stew.

1 Peel the butternut squash and cut it in half. Scoop out the seeds with a teaspoon and discard them, then cut the flesh into neat cubes. Set aside.

2 Make the chilli paste by pounding the shallots,

peppercorns, chilli and shrimp paste together using a mortar and pestle or by puréeing them in a spice blender.

3 Heat the stock, then add the chilli paste. Add the squash, beans and banana flower, if using. Simmer for about 15 minutes.

variation

Use pumpkin instead of butternut squash, or try acorn squash instead if you like.

4 Add the fish sauce, prawns and basil. Bring the soup to simmering point, then simmer for 3 minutes. Serve in four warmed bowls, accompanied by boiled rice.

cook's tip

Dried banana flowers are often available in Chinese or Asian supermarkets. The tender heart is good in salads.

NUTRITIONAL INFORMATION: Energy 68kcal/287kJ; Protein 11.2g; Carbohydrate 4.7g, of which sugars 3.4g; Fat 0.7g, of which saturates 0.2g; Cholesterol 110mg; Calcium 82mg; Fibre 1.7g; Sodium 108mg.

Coconut and Seafood Soup

The marriage of flavours works beautifully in this soup, which is easy to make.

ingredients

SERVES FOUR

- 600ml/1 pint/2½ cups fish stock
- 3 thin slices fresh root ginger
- 3 lemon grass stalks, chopped
- 3 kaffir lime leaves, shredded
- bunch of garlic chives, about 25g/1oz
- small bunch of fresh coriander (cilantro), about 15g/½oz
- 15ml/1 tbsp vegetable oil
- 4 shallots, chopped
- 400ml/14fl oz can coconut milk
- 30–45ml/2–3 tbsp fish sauce
- 45–60ml/3–4 tbsp green curry paste
- 450g/1lb raw large prawns (jumbo shrimp) peeled and deveined
- 450g/1lb prepared squid
- a little fresh lime juice (optional)
- salt and ground black pepper
- 60ml/4 tbsp crisp fried shallot slices, to serve

1 Pour the fish stock into a large pan and add the slices of ginger, the lemon grass and half the shredded lime leaves.

2 Reserve a few garlic chives for the garnish, then chop the remainder. Add half the chopped garlic chives to the pan. Strip the coriander leaves from the stalks and set the leaves aside. Add the stalks to the pan. Bring to the boil, reduce the heat to low and cover the pan, then simmer gently for 20 minutes. Strain the stock into a bowl.

3 Rinse and dry the pan. Add the oil and shallots. Cook for 5–10 minutes, until the shallots begin to turn golden.

4 Stir in the strained stock, coconut milk, the remaining lime leaves and 30ml/2 tbsp of the fish sauce. Heat gently until simmering and cook over a low heat for 5–10 minutes.

5 Stir in the curry paste and prawns, then cook for 3 minutes. Add the squid and cook for a further 2 minutes. Add the lime juice, if using, and season, adding more fish sauce to taste. Stir in the remaining chives and the reserved coriander leaves. Serve in bowls sprinkled with fried shallots and chives.

NUTRITIONAL INFORMATION: Energy 205kcal/871kJ; Protein 37.7g; Carbohydrate 7.5g, of which sugars 5.8g; Fat 3g, of which saturates 0.8g; Cholesterol 473mg; Calcium 144mg; Fibre 0.4g; Sodium 449mg.

Clear Soup with Seafood Sticks

This delicate Japanese soup, which is often eaten with sushi, is very quick to make.

ingredients

SERVES FOUR

- 4 mitsuba sprigs
  or 4 chives and a few sprigs
  of mustard and cress
- 4 seafood sticks
- 400ml/14fl oz/1⅔ cups
  first dashi stock, or the
  same amount of water
  and 5ml/1 tsp dashi-
  no-moto
- 15ml/1 tbsp shoyu (Japanese
  soy sauce)
- 7.5ml/1½ tsp salt
- grated rind of yuzu (optional),
  to garnish

1 Mitsuba leaves are normally sold with the stems and roots on to retain their freshness. First cut off the root, then cut 5cm/2in from the top, retaining both the long straw-like stem and the leaf.

2 Blanch the stems in hot water from the kettle. If you use chives, choose them at least 10cm/4in in length and blanch them, too.

3 Take a seafood stick and carefully tie around the middle with a mitsuba stem or chive, holding it in place with a knot. Do not pull too tightly, as the bow will easily break. Repeat to make four tied seafood sticks.

4 Hold one seafood stick in your hand. With your finger, carefully loosen both ends then fan the shreds out so that they look like tassels.

5 Arrange one seafood tassel in each of four soup bowls, then place the four mitsuba leaves or some mustard and cress on top of the seafood tassel.

6 Heat the dashi stock in a large pan and bring to the boil. Add the shoyu and salt. Pour the stock gently over the sprigs of mitsuba and seafood sticks among the four soup bowls. Sprinkle with grated yuzu rind to garnish, if using.

cook's tips

- *Mitsuba is a member of the parsley family and is available from Asian stores.*
- *You can make dashi stock by boiling a piece of kombu seaweed in water.*
- *Yuzu is a popular Japanese citrus fruit, about the same size as a clementine.*

NUTRITIONAL INFORMATION: Energy 9kcal/36kJ; Protein 1.1g; Carbohydrate 1g, of which sugars 0.3g; Fat 0.1g, of which saturates 0g; Cholesterol 4mg; Calcium 2mg; Fibre 0g; Sodium 1025mg.

COOK'S NOTES

Bracketed terms are intended for American readers.

For all recipes, quantities are given in both metric and imperial measures and, where appropriate, in standard cups and spoons. Follow one set of measures, but not a mixture, because they are not interchangeable.

Standard spoon and cup measures are level. 1 tsp = 5ml, 1 tbsp = 15ml, 1 cup = 250ml/8fl oz.

Australian standard tablespoons are 20ml. Australian readers should use 3 tsp in place of 1 tbsp for measuring small quantities.

American pints are 16fl oz/2 cups. American readers should use 20fl oz/2.5 cups in place of 1 pint when measuring liquids.

Electric oven temperatures in this book are for conventional ovens. When using a fan oven, the temperature will probably need to be reduced by about 10–20°C/20–40°F. Since ovens vary, you should check with your manufacturer's instruction book for guidance.

The nutritional analysis given for each recipe is calculated per portion (i.e. serving or item), unless otherwise stated. If the recipe gives a range, such as Serves 4–6, then the nutritional analysis will be for the smaller portion size, i.e. 6 servings. The analysis does not include optional ingredients, such as salt added to taste.

Medium (US large) eggs are used unless otherwise stated.

This edition is published by Lorenz Books,
an imprint of Anness Publishing Ltd,
Blaby Road, Wigston, Leicestershire, LE18 4SE

www.annesspublishing.com

If you like the images in this book and would like to investigate using them for publishing, promotions or advertising, please visit our website www.practicalpictures.com for more information.

© Anness Publishing Ltd 2012

A CIP catalogue record for this book is available from the British Library.